The Cambridge Introduction to
Shakespeare's Comedies

Why did theatre audiences laugh in Shakespeare's day and why do they
still laugh now? What did Shakespeare do with the conventions of
comedy that he inherited, so that his plays continue to amuse and move
audiences? What do his comedies have to say about love, sex, gender,
power, family, community, and class? What place have pain, cruelty, and
even death in a comedy? Why all those puns? In a survey that travels
from Shakespeare's earliest experiments in farce and courtly love-stories
to the great romantic comedies of his middle years and the
mould-breaking experiments of his last decade's work, this book
addresses these vital questions. Organised thematically, and covering all
Shakespeare's comedies from the beginning to the end of his career, it
provides readers with a map of the playwright's comic styles, showing
how he built on comedic conventions as he further enriched the
possibilities of the genre.

PENNY GAY is Professor of English and Drama at the University of
Sydney.

Cambridge Introductions to Literature

This series is designed to introduce students to key topics and authors. Accessible and lively, these introductions will also appeal to readers who want to broaden their understanding of the books and authors they enjoy.

- Ideal for students, teachers, and lecturers
- Concise, yet packed with essential information
- Key suggestions for further reading

Titles in this series

The Cambridge Introduction to
Shakespeare's Comedies

PENNY GAY

CAMBRIDGE
UNIVERSITY PRESS

CAMBRIDGE UNIVERSITY PRESS
Cambridge, New York, Melbourne, Madrid, Cape Town, Singapore, São Paulo, Delhi

Cambridge University Press
The Edinburgh Building, Cambridge CB2 8RU, UK

Published in the United States of America by Cambridge University Press, New York

www.cambridge.org
Information on this title: www.cambridge.org/9780521672696

First published 2008

Printed in the United Kingdom at the University Press, Cambridge

A catalogue record for this publication is available from the British Library

Library of Congress Cataloging-in-Publication Data
Gay, Penny, 1945–
The Cambridge introduction to Shakespeare's comedies / Penny Gay.
    p.   cm. – (Cambridge introductions to literature)
Includes bibliographical references and index.
ISBN 978-0-521-85668-3 (hardback) – ISBN 978-0-521-67269-6 (pbk.)
1. Shakespeare, William, 1564–1616 – Comedies.   2. English drama (Comedy) – History
and criticism.   I. Title.   III. Series.
PR2981.G39   2008
822.3′3 – dc22   2007050651

ISBN 978-0-521-85668-3 hardback
ISBN 978-0-521-67269-6 paperback

Contents

Preface

Why did audiences laugh in Shakespeare's day, why do they still laugh now? What did Shakespeare do with the conventions of comedy that he inherited, so that his plays continue to amuse and move audiences? What do his comedies have to say about love, sex, gender, power, family, community, and class? What place have pain, cruelty, and even death in a comedy? Why all those puns?

These questions have fascinated me for at least thirty years of my professional life. I am grateful to Sarah Stanton for the opportunity finally to explore them and to begin to map out their connections. I must also thank my colleagues at the University of Sydney, particularly the members of the Early Modern Literature and Culture group, for providing clues and answers to odd matters. Kirsten Tranter was an imaginative and thorough research assistant, and I have enjoyed many illuminating conversations with drama specialists Kate Flaherty and Margaret Rogerson.

My daughter Virginia Gay read the whole book from the double perspective of Shakespeare enthusiast and professional actress; I am profoundly grateful for her insights and her insistence on clarity. As my test reader, she kept me to the book's aim: simply to help twenty-first-century readers, theatre-goers, and actors find their bearings and increase their enjoyment of plays which – as Duke Theseus says – 'need no excuse'.

Quotations from Shakespeare's plays are from the individual editions of the New Cambridge Shakespeare, wherever possible; other editions, where used, are indicated in the notes.

Chapter 1

Introduction: comedy as idea and practice

Laughter

Laughter is universal; we all need to laugh, and many different events can bring it about. Throughout the sixteenth century there were significant discussions of the role of laughter in relation to the 'decorum' – or proper conduct – of daily life, especially among the gentry and nobility, who were considered the patterns of Renaissance behaviour. Here is one such discussion:

> He is a living creature that can laugh: because this laughing is perceived only in man, and (in manner) always is a token of a certain jocundness and merry mood that he feeleth inwardly in his mind, which by nature is drawn to pleasantness and coveteth quietness and refreshing, for which cause we can see men have invented many matters, as sports, games and pastimes, and so many sundry sorts of open shows . . .
>
> And although all kind of jests move a man to laugh, yet do they also in this laughter make diverse effects. For some have in them a certain cleanness and modest pleasantness. Other bite sometime privily, otherwhile openly. Other have in them a certain wantonness. Other make one laugh as soon as he heareth them. Other the more a man thinketh upon them. Other in laughing make a man blush withal. Other stir a man somewhat to anger. But in all kinds a man must consider the disposition of the minds of the hearers.
>
> Baldassare Castiglione, *The Book of the Courtier*, tr. Thomas Hoby (1561), Book 2

What is the relation between laughter and comedy? It will be the business of this book to tease out the distinction, to look at the ways in which Shakespeare, writing in the 1590s and the first decade of the 1600s, combined laughter-causing moments with a form of dramatic story-telling that has a long and ancient history. Whatever happens along the way in a dramatic comedy, the ending will offer an image of happiness – for at least some of the characters whose fortunes we have followed. If for others there is sadness and exclusion, that is a reminder that comedy's optimism is an artificial and selective view of the world (just as tragedy's pessimism is). Shakespeare plays many variations on the mix of laughter and sadness within the form of comedy – and productions of these plays can opt for greatly different moods and emphases. One constant, however, is the practice of clowning: the contribution of actors whose job it is to amuse the audience – hopefully, to make them laugh – at various points in the play.

When Castiglione speaks of 'the disposition of the minds of the hearers' he is reminding us of the most vital aspect of comedy: its audience. His list of 'jests' acknowledges that things strike us as funny in different ways at different times. Yet in writing a comedy, the playwright must provide the opportunity for clowns to do their work. To begin, then, with a question: what is the funniest Shakespeare scene you (the reader) can recall in performance, either professional or amateur? Most people, without having to think much, will enthusiastically offer the performance of the play 'Pyramus and Thisbe' in the last act of *A Midsummer Night's Dream*. After this, three other comic models often come to mind: Malvolio's letter scene and cross-gartered appearance before Olivia (*Twelfth Night*); Beatrice and Benedick's volley of sarcastic put-downs and their 'overhearing' scenes (*Much Ado About Nothing*); and – my personal favourite – the one-sided conversations between Lance and his oblivious dog in *Two Gentlemen of Verona*.

What is it about these scenes (and their analogues) that almost infallibly produces laughter when played on a stage? (though it may very well not do so in silent reading). Between them, like Castiglione's list, they create a rough taxonomy of types of comic *events*, or 'business'.

(1) The play-scene in *A Midsummer Night's Dream*, in which the 'rude mechanicals', 'hard-handed men' with little or no formal education, take on the performance of a classical tragedy, as written (it seems likely) by Peter Quince. They know how tragedy is supposed to go, with high passions expressed in elaborate metaphors, a hopeless love, and a drawn-out death scene. Nick Bottom, who plays the hero Pyramus – and would happily play all the other parts – believes profoundly in his own gifts as an actor, and the importance of getting the story told with maximum effect. In fact, he and his companions are a little 'afeared' of theatre's potential to stir feeling, to convince the audience that what is happening on stage is 'real'; so various prologues, explanations, and interruptions are scripted into the play to reassure the audience. Each of the actors takes his role in telling the story with immense seriousness: Snout (Wall) as the first-act 'set', very important as the symbol of separation of the lovers; Starveling (Moonshine) as the 'lights', a role often under-appreciated in the theatre, as Starveling is made mortifyingly aware; Snug (Lion), anxious to let all know he is no villain really, but 'a very gentle beast' – his role is of course vital, for without

him there would be no tragedy of misunderstanding. Then there are the eloquent hero and heroine, each of whom has a dithyrambic death scene, Thisbe's ending the play with such self-believing passion (Flute never steps out of role to explain it) that it often silences the patronising on stage audience and wrings a tear. This brief analysis suggests that the play-scene is funny because its situation is so familiar to everyone in the audience: the community recognises its own passion for drama, and laughs, not in contempt like the on stage audience, but in delighted acknowledgement of that irrational need – and of the courage of the actors who would respond to it, whatever absurdity that may involve.

(2) Malvolio's letter scene, and its follow-up, the cross-gartered scene, represents the classic come-down of a self-important figure – the banana-skin joke. Here we laugh, as Hobbes said, because of a 'sudden glory':

> Laughter is nothing else but sudden glory arising from some sudden conception of some eminency in ourselves, by comparison with the infirmity of others, or with our own formerly.
>
>   Thomas Hobbes, *Human Nature* (1650), ch. 9

We might gloss this by adding that we sense that the world is momentarily just and has punished the overweening by making them *look* funny. As early as 1602 law student John Manningham noted his enjoyment of this aspect of *Twelfth Night*: 'a good practice in it to make the steward believe his lady widow was in love with him, by counterfeiting a letter as from his lady, in general terms telling him what she liked best in him, and prescribing his gesture in smiling, his apparel, etc., and then when he came to practise, making him believe they took him to be mad'.[1]

(3) The gulling of Benedick, making him believe that Beatrice loves him, is another version of the Malvolio joke: his reactions to the set-up scene (he has to pretend he's not there, 'overhearing' his friends) provide opportunities for great physical comedy. Some Beatrices go the same way in their parallel scene, seeking laughter by excessive mugging as she listens, but as I shall argue in chapter 5, the style of the text suggests a more serious reading of this scene. On the other hand, the several scenes between Beatrice and Benedick, right up to the last moments of the play, are full of attempts by each to outdo the other in sarcasm, and they can be very funny if the actors invest them with enough venom.

(4) Lance and his dog, in *Two Gentlemen* 2.3, 2.5, and 4.4. As Lance delivers two brilliant stand-up monologues (2.3, 4.4), the dog, who is partly the subject of them, does whatever dogs do (or whatever an actor in a dog-suit thinks will get a laugh). The joke here is the demonstration

(without danger) before our eyes of the absurd uncontrollability of the natural world in which we live.

To these examples of what is basically *visual* comedy (that is, the undermining of seriously intended speech with bodily incongruities or indignity), we can add some specifically *aural* laughter-producing mechanisms, when a character mangling and misapplying the English language tickles the collective funnybone because of his departure from the norm.[2] Don Armado's extraordinarily florid utterances sound even weirder when delivered in a Spanish accent – in fact, most accents that are not London or the home counties are automatically funny to English ears. Dogberry's, Elbow's, Mistress Quickly's, and others' malapropisms frequently produce an unintentional indecency (the Latin lesson in *Merry Wives* 4.1 is a virtuoso example); they have the same laughter-producing effect as an unrepressed fart or belch. They remind us that we are all ultimately comic, i.e. potentially grotesque bodies, and that decorum cannot or should not be always maintained.

> The place therefore and (as it were) the headspring that laughing matters arise of, consisteth in a certain deformity or ill favouredness, because a man laugheth only at those matters that are disagreeing in themselves, and (to a man's seeming) are in ill plight, where it is not so in deed . . . to make men laugh always is not comely for the Courtier, nor yet in such wise as frantic, drunken, foolish and fond [silly] men and in like manner common jesters do: and though to a man's thinking Courts cannot be without such kind of persons, yet deserve they not the name of a Courtier.
>
> Castiglione, *The Courtier* (tr. Hoby), Book 2

Castiglione understands that laughter is necessary to mental health, and he is aware – perhaps grateful – that there are people who can be employed professionally to provide this. He is consistently anxious (as the rest of his discussion makes clear) about the tendency of the educated gentry to imitate the witty 'jests' and 'merry pranks' of the professional performers. This ambivalence can be found in many of Shakespeare's depictions of young men – perhaps most strikingly in the comedy that turns to tragedy, *Romeo and Juliet*. Shakespeare's clowns, however, never doubt their right and ability to make a joke.

Comic models

Beyond laughter and jesting, for both performers and audiences in the theatre, comedy exists as a narrative form or structure. This form is based on the expectation that the delightful temporary disorder of the tale will be resolved with reincorporation into normal society – or at least a gesture towards that: a gesture that can be, on occasion, deeply ironical. Comedies, as a genre, end with weddings and feasts rather than deaths and funerals – though the latter can often be sensed not too far away.

Models of comic structure were provided in the pre-Shakespearean English theatre via a number of routes:

(1) Roman comedy, the plays of Terence and Plautus, were used in schools to teach Latin, even though their plots usually displayed the 'immoral' triumph of the young lovers, aided by clever servants, over the foolish father-figures. Shakespeare's *Comedy of Errors* is an adaptation of Plautus' *Menaechmi*: he outdoes his master by adding, among other plot elements, another pair of twins to the Antipholi – their comic servants the Dromios. Other character-types that occur in Roman comedy and are picked up by Shakespeare in various plays include the boastful soldier, the doctor (either as conman or foolish old man), and the shrewish wife.

(2) These comic types were developed in sixteenth-century Italian comedy: both what was called *commedia erudita* (literary comedy played in aristo- cratic courts and academies and widely published) and *commedia dell'arte*, the work of travelling playing companies that 'ransacked the literary plays for materials for their improvised three-act scenarios or for their own occa- sional five-act scripted plays'.[3] Some commedia companies (with their adult women players) visited England in Shakepeare's lifetime, and his energetic use of the commedia style in, for example, *The Taming of the Shrew* sug- gests his possible acquaintance with a theatrical example rather than just travellers' reports, or a reading of published scenarios. The major collec- tion of commedia scenarios was published (in Italian) in 1611, too late for Shakespeare to make specific use of them; yet they clearly, as Louise Clubb writes,

> memorialize several decades of experience in the Italian professional theatre and demonstrate much of its range. They attest to a continual mining of the kinds of fictive material also used by Shakespeare and to a method of selecting, combining and disposing stageworthy elements from a shared repertory . . . common among them are errors involving twins; the bed trick in a dark room; disguise of sex or social condition in order to serve a beloved, often entailing carrying messages to a new love and becoming the object of his or her affections; revelations of identity and reunions of separated families; tricks to fleece misers and to mock would-be seducers, presumptuous wooers and fortune-hunters; madness and pretended madness; supposed death.[4]

(3) In the mid-1580s the English writers John Lyly and George Peele wrote and published highly literary plays that were performed at court and read by fashionable ladies. Janette Dillon writes, 'It is with Lyly that the exploration of love and its effects on lovers begins. We find the musings of lovers on their own feelings, the mockery of their folly by others, the careful plotting of the game of love . . . Lyly also anticipates Shakespeare in providing witty minor characters who indulge in extended repartee . . . wordplay and chop-logic.'[5]

The stage was now set for Shakespearean comedy.

Shakespeare and comedy

Shakespeare's major comedies were written at a peculiarly fertile time in English cultural history: the 1590s. The professional public theatre was flourishing (purpose-built theatres had only appeared in London in the 1570s); London was a rich melting-pot of people of all classes; printed books were becoming cheap and popular; artistic and philosophical discussions were fashionable, but so were gossip, travellers' tales, and stories of the teeming underlife of the city. 'Mongrel' theatre (as Sir Philip Sidney called it – see below), or hybrid forms, would seem to suit the very temper of the times.

In general, there was already a strong tradition of 'miscellaneity' in the earlier English drama; Janette Dillon lists examples of plays that were successfully given at court. Thomas Preston's *King Cambises* (c. 1558–69), for example, 'has a title page describing it as "a Lamentable Tragedie, mixt full of plesant mirth"'.[6] So Theseus in *A Midsummer Night's Dream*, commenting on the 'very tragical mirth' offered by 'Pyramus and Thisbe', should be well used to the mixed genre, and although he finds it amusingly naïve, unlike Egeus (or Sidney), he appreciates the work of 'imagination' and of 'simpleness and duty' – the humility of the actors in making their offering.

There were objections, both moral and intellectual. The anti-theatricalist Stephen Gosson wrote in *Plays Confuted* in 1582, that 'bawdy Comedies in Latin, French, Italian, and Spanish, have been thoroughly ransacked to furnish the playhouses in London'. He was simply recording a fact: that professional English theatre was in its early heyday, and writers and owners of the theatres were energetically availing themselves of anything that could be adapted and would sell to an audience. As well as the long tradition of moralising against the theatre, here represented by Gosson, there was also aesthetic criticism. Sir Philip Sidney's famous complaint in his *Apology for Poetry* is typical:

all their plays be neither right tragedies, nor right comedies, mingling kings and clowns, not because the matter so carrieth it, but thrust in clowns by head and shoulders, to play a part in majestical matters, with neither decency nor discretion, so as neither the admiration and commiseration, nor the right sportfulness, is by their mongrel tragi-comedy obtained.

Sir Philip Sidney, *Apology for Poetry* (written c. 1579–80, published 1595)

Sidney was an aristocrat and a poet; his perspective comes from his classical education – and he wrote well before Shakespeare began his career. At the centre of his argument is the theory of decorum, or fitness, which is to be found in all the major theoretical treatises of the sixteenth century, for example Castiglione (quoted above). As Viola remarks after her conversation with Feste about the job of being a jester: 'He must observe their mood on whom he jests, / The quality of persons, and the time . . .' (3.1.50–4).[7]

As for a witty man, so for a play, goes the classical theory. But the popular and successful plays of the sixteenth century got their laughs and their popular success by being *in*decorous, by combining 'kings and clowns', just as Shakespeare went on to do; miracles and rough magic; grotesque bodies and graceful heroics. Imogen's lament (*Cymbeline* 4.2) over the decapitated body of Cloten, which she thinks to be that of her husband, is an extreme example of this teasing and disruption of the audience's responses by refusing to obey the rules of decorum: actresses performing this scene never know whether they will get laughter or sympathetic, suspenseful silence. The scene was anticipated more than ten years earlier, in Thisbe's lament over Pyramus in the Mechanicals' play (*Dream* 5.1), with verbal cues suggesting a comic response. But even here, a determined Flute/Thisbe can silence laughter by the intensity of 'her' performance.

The same effects can be found in the English vernacular tradition of drama that Shakespeare knew: the Mystery plays, dating from the fifteenth century when England was still a Catholic country and the church engaged the imagination of the people through the annual amateur drama festivals that re-told the narratives of the Christian faith. The Annunciation play (often known as 'Joseph's Trouble about Mary') always gets a laugh on Joseph's line 'Who hath been here since I went?' as he points at Mary's heavily pregnant belly. Mak the sheep-stealer in the *Second Shepherd's Play* (telling of the birth of the Christ child) is a clever conman who finally gets his comeuppance, tossed in a blanket.

In the Morality plays of the fifteenth and early sixteenth centuries, in which allegorical figures such as Everyman underwent moral and religious adventures, the figure of the 'Vice' became prominent. The Vice (he has various names in different plays) represents the attractive face of wrong-doing: he is cleverer than anyone else on stage; he chats to the audience about how he is going to fool everyone with his tricks, thus making the audience complicit. He almost always gets found out, so that the audience has learnt a lesson – however clever or superior they think they are, ultimately goodness and righteousness will win. Shakespeare models his blackly comic Richard III on the Vice, and develops it further in much later plays – Iago in *Othello*, Iachimo in *Cymbeline*. But arguably, the Vice's habit of witty chat to the audience, his penchant for turning up unexpectedly – and taking advantage of the situation – influence the development of the Shakespearean clown.

Clowns

It is important to distinguish between the several types of clown on the Elizabethan stage. The servant (e.g. the Dromios of *The Comedy of Errors*) is a figure derived from Roman comedy and its sixteenth-century Italian descendants, notably in the *commedia dell'arte*. This type of clown indulges in witty exchanges with his master and others, but is also subject to constant physical abuse, though the genre of farce can make this seem merely comical. I discuss this type of comedy in chapter 2.

The country clown is a creation of the English native tradition – a sweet-natured but unsophisticated figure, whose view of the world is entirely restricted to his local activities. He can be witty, but it is more often an accident than a deliberately professional attempt to hold the intellectual high ground. Costard in *Love's Labour's Lost* is an excellent early example of this type (his exit line in 3.1 about the monetary difference between a 'remuneration' and a 'guerdon' always gets a laugh); and he is still to be found in the delightful Young Shepherd of *The Winter's Tale*, conned out of his money by the Vice or 'rogue', Autolycus.

A variant of this type is the non-rural worker: he may be the community constable (Dogberry, Dull, Elbow); he may be the castle porter (*Macbeth*); he may be a pimp (Pompey in *Measure for Measure*) or a grave-digger (*Hamlet*). Although these roles may simply be classified as 'comic', they function – as do the country clowns – as satirical commentators on the doings of the higher folk.

It is this commentary role, whether conscious or unintentional, that is at the heart of the clown's function. It acts a bridge between stage and audience. The Fool, the most consciously witty of Shakespeare's clown roles (always played by a specialist actor in Shakespeare's company), is a professional jester, who makes his living by begging tips for his jokes and songs; he is usually attached to a noble household, though he may not actually live there. His role is to deflate, through wit (at times obscure, perhaps deliberately so), the more pretentious attitudes of those in power. In *Twelfth Night* 3.1 Feste draws our attention to this role in his conversation with Viola; in *As You Like It* Touchstone's 'moralising' job is greatly envied by Jaques, himself a somewhat sardonic outsider; in *All's Well* Lavatch foregrounds his relation to the audience by satirising the fawning behaviour of courtiers in his virtuoso 'I have an answer that will serve all men . . . "O Lord, sir!"'(2.2). All stand aslant to the society on which they depend. In the course of this discussion of Shakespeare's comedies, I will be suggesting that often the heroines take on a double role, as another Fool, chatting wittily to the audience about their situation and their position as outsiders to the powerful (and patriarchal) court.

Actors

The French word for actor is *comédien*; it began to be used about the middle of the sixteenth century, 'indicat[ing] a general sense of a new form of entertainment or a new type of occupation'; professional acting, in short.[8] Olivia asks Viola (disguised as Cesario) at their first meeting, 'Are you a comedian?' Viola replies equivocally, 'No, my profound heart; and yet, by the very fangs of malice, I swear, I am not that I play' (*Twelfth Night* 1.5.151–3). This exchange sets up one of the most persistent themes of Shakespearean comedy: its metatheatrical consciousness. Like a number of his contemporary playwrights, Shakespeare does not want the audience to lose themselves in the story to the degree that they forget that they are in a theatre. This awareness, these plays suggest, actually adds to their pleasure – the audience, trained and sophisticated by decades of public theatre, becomes a privileged assistant to the actors' job of story-telling.

Actors were nevertheless, at this time, legally 'vagabonds', having virtually no rights in the social structure. The safest way around this situation was to become a member of a company of players attached to a nobleman or member of the court. Shakespeare's company began as the Lord Chamberlain's Men, and mutated triumphantly into the King's Men on the accession of James I. This position gave them a modicum of protection from prosecution, but it also put them in the position of having to keep their patron on side. The role of the Clown has thus a particular resonance: because he is 'an allowed fool' (*Twelfth Night* 1.5.76), and an accomplished verbal quibbler, he is the locus of any satirical protest that the successful, commercial company – operating in its own theatre well away from both court and puritanical city – might want to express against their feudal situation.

Audiences and spaces

This somewhat constrained situation is echoed in a peculiarity of Shakespeare's plays. Fictional 'theatrical performances' – plays within plays – always have an aristocratic audience: the Mechanicals play before Theseus and Hippolyta in *A Midsummer Night's Dream*; the rustics play for the King of Navarre and the Princess of France and their lords and ladies (*Love's Labour's Lost*); the Players play for Claudius' court in *Hamlet*. In reality, most performances of Shakespeare's plays were in the public theatre, where audiences were of all sorts and conditions of men – and women. Aristocrats and gentlemen would also visit the purpose-built outdoor theatres, sitting perhaps in the 'Lords' room' above the stage or the 'gentlemen's rooms' in the first bays next to the stage. The rest of the theatre held a mixed audience, from the 'groundlings' standing around the thrust stage – and able to get right up to its edge and make their presence felt – to those sitting or standing in the three storeys of covered galleries.[9] The reproduction Shakespeare's Globe on London's South Bank provides a wonderful modern experience of the actor–audience relationship in all parts of the theatre – though most scholars now agree that the building itself is too big, and the placing and size of the stage pillars remains controversial.

All Shakespeare's plays had to be viable for touring, or for performing at court, in a college hall, in a great country house, or in the indoor hall theatres increasingly built after the turn of the century. They were written with these conditions in mind: 'plays were performed with a minimum of scenic and mechanical aids, in costumes whose lavishness would surprise us more than it surprised the first audiences . . . Disguise flourishes on such a stage, because it stands out, and because the audience is interested in clothes.'[10] Peter Thomson further points out that 'Timid acting has no chance in such a setting. The Elizabethan actor, if he was to be effective, must have determined to dominate both the platform and the surrounding audience' (43).

This is a space for actors to fill with their energy; it cannot depend on scenery or lighting for its effects. At times the stage will be full of actors – for example, in the opening scene or the masked dance scene (2.1) of *Much Ado About Nothing*: out of this crowd first one group of speakers, then another, will emerge to focus the audience's attention; and thus, this play's themes of gossip, rumour, overhearing are made visible for the audience. Or the stage may hold just two or three speakers, in dialogue, or even one, in soliloquy. At all points the actors' responsibility is to use the dramaturgy to tell the play's story. In the case of soliloquies, the potential arises for the solo actor to breach the stage–audience divide and share his or her thoughts and comments with that other source of energy, the audience.

Robert Weimann has proposed that the stage space of the Elizabethan and Jacobean theatre can be thought of as divided, in terms of dramaturgy and the audience's perception, into *locus* and *platea*. The *locus* is

> a fairly specific imaginary locale or self-contained space in the world of
> the play[;] and the *platea* [is] an opening in *mise-en-scène* through
> which the place and time of the stage-as-stage and the cultural occasion
> itself are made either to assist or resist the socially and verbally elevated,
> spatially and temporally remote representation.[11]

In simpler terms, we might think of 'story' versus 'commentary'. In the *locus*, the story's imaginary locale, characters who are entirely absorbed in their (fictional) lives play out their high-sounding, often literary sentiments. Such scenes are often played centre-stage or upstage, well away from the audience. Near to or on the edge of the stage – the *platea*, which can include the audience space – the clowns and other comedic characters perform for and comment knowingly to the audience; they move freely into and out of the story, taking their awareness of the audience with them. Shakespearean comedy often makes significant use of this 'opening' or intersection between stage and audience. The first three scenes of *Twelfth Night* are a good example of such varied dramaturgy. Two scenes establish the poles of the romantic fable – the self-absorbed Count Orsino and the destitute Viola; and then there follows a scene introducing the roisterers, Sir Toby and company, who have not a care in the world except to entertain themselves (and by extension, the audience). Sir Andrew's over-the-top performance as the scene ends – the dancing clown, with his onstage audience Sir Toby urging him on – clearly marks this element of the play as belonging to the *platea*.

Comedy, that is, tends to inhabit a liminal space (one on the edge, either literally or metaphorically), a place between *locus* and audience. It rarely forgets that there is an audience; and it posits the liminal position as one that bestows the sort of power that arises from resistance to authority, whether that be social or literary. (Authority is of course always complicit with the theory of decorum.) The audience, originally in the same lighting conditions as the actors, is made conscious of its role as listeners and watchers, and is thus invited into the stage's community, in a similar position to the liminal characters in the world of the play. The potentially most interesting characters, therefore, will be those who move flexibly between *locus* and *platea* – the 'old Vice' as Feste calls him (*Twelfth Night* 4.2.106), all clowns, and many of the heroines.

In looking at Shakespearean comedy, this book will always consider the plays as texts written with this lively and alert audience in mind – an audience who are familiar with old models of tales and characters, who expect clowns (and song), but who are willing to be surprised by what happens to and through these elements. As Janette Dillon argues, 'While [Shakespeare's] plays so evidently grow out of English stage traditions . . . their characteristic attitude towards tradition is dialogic, playful, and exploratory. That conscious dialogism works by constructing an audience alert to allusions, quotations, and in-jokes.'[12]

Modern theories of comedy

For many decades, in the history of Shakespearean criticism, the comedies were largely ignored. The dramatic genres of tragedy and, to a lesser extent, history deal with issues that are of importance to a culture that is basically patriarchal and nationalistic, such as that of Europe since at least the first millennium. In the middle of the twentieth century a different mode of critical discussion developed, based on work by anthropologists and historians who were newly studying the life of the ordinary people in a community. Attention turned to the idea of *carnival*, the folk feasts of 'misrule' that were common in medieval and Renaissance Europe: those occasions on which a period of topsy-turvydom was allowed by the authorities (Mardi Gras, the period just before Lent, is perhaps the most persistent of these festivals). Servants could ape their masters in processions, feasts, and dances; normal rules of decorum were bibulously flouted; the body's demands for food, sex, and relaxation were indulged to the maximum. In a few days it would all be over, and the workers would return to their frugal and oppressed lives until the next holiday.

These developments in the critical idea of community had a profound effect on a generation of Shakespearean critics; they provided a new tool for understanding the persistence and attraction of the comedies. C. L. Barber, in *Shakespeare's Festive Comedy* (1959), argued that Shakespeare

> used the resources of a sophisticated theatre to express, in his idyllic comedies and in his clowns' ironic misrule, the experience of moving to humorous understanding through saturnalian release . . .
>
> A saturnalian attitude, assumed by a clear-cut gesture toward liberty, brings mirth, an accession of wanton vitality. In the terms of Freud's

analysis of wit, the energy normally occupied in maintaining inhibition is freed for celebration . . .

The *clarification* achieved by the festive comedies is concomitant to the release they dramatize: a heightened awareness of the relation between man and 'nature' – the nature celebrated on holiday . . . The plays present a mockery of what is unnatural.[13]

Northrop Frye, less interested in anthropology and more interested in mythology and literary structure, offered this not dissimilar version of the enduring power of the comedies:

The tendency of the comic society to include rather than exclude is the reason for the traditional importance of the parasite, who has no business to be at the final festival but is nevertheless there. The word 'grace', with all its Renaissance overtones from the graceful courtier of Castiglione to the gracious God of Christianity, is a most important thematic word for Shakespearean comedy . . .

Shakespeare's type of romantic comedy follows a tradition . . . which has affinities with the medieval tradition of the seasonal ritual-play. We may call it the drama of the green world, its plot being assimilated to the ritual theme of the triumph of life and love over the waste land . . . in all these comedies there is the same rhythmic movement from normal world to green world and back again.[14]

The patterns proposed by Frye and Barber do work, by and large; they remain a useful first approach to 'meaning' in many of these plays. But, as Jean Howard points out,

reliance on certain premises of Frye and Barber can lead us to minimize some aspects of the comedies, most notably the degree of unresolved turbulence and contradiction present in those plays and present in the audience's aesthetic experience of them . . . even the festive comedies frequently function as problem-posing structures that produce aesthetic experiences marked as much by rupture and discontinuity as by the serene harmonization of contradictory elements.[15]

Critics in the 1980s and 1990s looked again at Shakespeare's plays, from the generally political perspectives provided by feminism and 'new' historicism. Pioneering research established the meanings these apparently light comedies might have carried for a contemporary audience (for example, the issue of landowners forcing out tenant farmers in order to enclose their land, which underlies life in the forest of Arden in *As You Like It*). Many of these investigations can provide interesting political parallels today if directors wish to set the plays in modern dress; for example, it is easy to see that *Measure for Measure* is deeply interested in abuses of power, whether it be by a Duke and his deputy, or an absent CEO and his sexually uptight second-in-command.

Two hours' traffic

A good production of a comedy can grip the imagination just as thoroughly as the most famous tragedies and histories. Comedies can provide meaningful stories, as well as opportunities for laughter and relaxation. Only a third of the way through Shakespeare's playwriting career a contemporary play-goer noted Shakespeare's 'excellence' in both comedy and tragedy:

> for comedy witness his *Gentlemen of Verona*, his *Errors*, his *Love Labours Lost*, his *Love Labours Won*,[16] his *Midsummer Night's Dream* and his *Merchant of Venice*.
>
> Francis Meres, *Palladis Tamia: Wits Treasury* (1598)

Modern scholars do not disagree with this catalogue of comedies (though they add, as does the Folio, *The Taming of the Shrew* from this early period). After examining these 'excellent' plays, this book follows Shakespeare to the end of his writing career, looking at the group of comedies that followed 1598 – *The Merry Wives of Windsor, Much Ado About Nothing, As You Like It, Twelfth Night* – and then at his continuing use of elements of comedy in plays written in the new century: *Measure for Measure, All's Well that Ends Well, Cymbeline, The Winter's Tale*, and *The Tempest*. In these later plays, romance, clowning, and comic situations don't disappear: they are just embedded in a much darker fable.

Although I have grouped plays roughly chronologically and generically or thematically, the focus of every discussion is each play's overall effect as a story told in the theatre. It is important to attend to the timing and weight of individual scenes: what happens at what stage, in relation to what, and how much stage time and energy is given to it. In the prologue to that comi-tragedy, *Romeo and Juliet*, the Chorus refers to 'the two hours' traffic of our stage.' Plays take place in time, and in a confined space: the audience is captive, but it is also expecting to be entertained. In terms of dramaturgical excellence, therefore, any play must hit certain sweet spots. The opening scene must engage our attention, and set up not only a situation but also some aspect of the theme that will be explored through language: the latter usually operates subconsciously, so that at later moments in the play certain words, ideas, metaphors, will evoke a 'chime'.

These thematic issues will often be brought to the fore in a scene, usually in Act 3, which is not strictly necessary to the plot, but allows for a moment of reflection by the audience. Good examples can be found in the conversation between Feste and Viola (*Twelfth Night* 3.1, quoted above); Shylock's 'Hath not a Jew eyes?' speech (*The Merchant of Venice* 3.1); and Benedick's and Beatrice's soliloquies at the end of their 'gulling' scenes (*Much Ado*): 'This can be no trick! . . . The world must be peopled' (2.3), 'What fire is in mine ears! Can this be true?' (3.1.). The end, when it finally and satisfyingly comes, will discharge all ignorance and misunderstanding (the moment of *anagnorisis*), will bring together those who deserve to be so, in marriage or family reconciliation, and will punish the evil-doer, but in a way that suggests the wish that even he may be redeemed in time. Marriages and reunions, not death and disharmony, characterise the end of a Shakespearean comedy, though disharmony can never be completely ruled out in the sublunary world.

What, irreducibly, does the audience experience in the two hours' traffic of a Shakespearean comedy? A sense that they have had the 'holiday' of living in another world; of experiencing others' lives and problems with the assurance that most of them will be resolved happily at the play's end; of sharing a sense of the laughable absurdities of the ordinary world which can't be fixed. As Castiglione wrote, 'Whatsoever therefore causeth laughter, the same maketh the mind jocund and giveth pleasure, nor suffereth a man in that instant to mind the troublesome griefs that our life is full of. Therefore (as you see) laughing is very acceptable to all men, and he is much to be commended that can cause it in due time and after a comely sort.'

Chapter 2

Farce

When we use the theatrical term 'farce' today we usually understand it to mean 'French farce', or 'sex comedy': plays set in bedrooms or drawing-rooms with lots of doors and hiding spaces for adults attempting to engage in illicit sex. This type of drama works via a frenetic pace and split-second comic timing. The *Oxford Dictionary of English* (2nd edn, 2005) defines farce as 'a comic dramatic work using buffoonery and horseplay and typically including crude characterisation and ludicrously improbable situations'. From the French cooking term, *farcir*, to stuff, in the early sixteenth century the word 'became used metaphorically for comic interludes "stuffed" into the texts of religious plays . . . "suche as writte farcis and contrefait [counterfeit] the vulgare speche"' (as translator Jehan Palsgrave wrote in 1530). If there is sexual activity, that is, it's not necessarily the most important driver of the play, and it certainly doesn't represent the behaviour of upper-class people.

Horseplay, buffoonery, vulgarity (including really crude sex jokes, often visual, involving oversize phalluses) – all are important defining aspects of comedy pre-Shakespeare. Words are often less important than actions, and because of this physicality there's always a possibility of violence in this type of theatre. It's intriguing to speculate why this is so: might there be a clue in that early concept of farce? If the reality of life in this world is, as Thomas Hobbes said in 1651, 'poor, nasty, brutish, and short', and we live in 'continual fear and danger of violent death' (Hobbes, *Leviathan*, ch. 13), the church-going members of the medieval community might have welcomed the 'stuffing' of this perception into a pious religious play that exhorts us to behave ourselves and look to our heavenly reward – or punishment. They had to laugh, because there was no way out of this stark medieval model: heaven or hell. But under the Renaissance humanist model that was Shakespeare's intellectual environment, there is a possibility of 'heaven on earth': a society based on civility, the resolution of problems by the application of reason and good will, marriage based on romantic love; and central to all, the importance of the arts as a sign of the human drive towards order and beauty.

Shakespeare was yet to develop the new model of romantic comedy, but G. K. Hunter's subtle analysis of the characteristics of Shakespearean farce indicates an aesthetic connection, a link to the world of romance (which I explore further in chapters 3 and 5):

> The mode of farce . . . is one in which the complex of plot and character is dominated by its plot aspect, so that characters are shown making a series of ad hoc assertions of self against the dominant process of social events moving inexorably through time . . . The unceasing and manic energy of farce in these plays comes from their central characters' unrelenting determination to reject complicity with the world around them. But . . . [t]he unity of the play's world demands that the opponents finally admit that they belong to one another . . . It is necessarily late in the action when the protagonists discover that complicity is possible and rewarding. But the audience has always known this.[1]

In relation to Shakespeare's two earliest comedies, *The Comedy of Errors* and *The Taming of the Shrew* (both 1592–4), we can see this pattern energetically at work. We can also trace the typically sixteenth-century hybridisation of earlier forms of dramatic comedy that would have been familiar to the young playwright.

There were two major forms of English medieval religious drama, both of which utilised comic characters and farcical behaviour within their serious and didactic fables. The 'mystery play' cycles, stories from the Bible, from Creation to Last Judgement, were performed on a fairly regular annual basis in some towns by the local guilds (of trades such as shoemakers, goldsmiths, etc.). Coventry, which had one such cycle, was just up the road from Stratford-upon-Avon, and its cycle was still being played in the 1570s – the last known performance was in 1579 – despite bans from the Protestant government. We can imagine the young Shakespeare going to Coventry to see some of these performances. There were also the 'morality plays' or 'interludes' performed by strolling actors' companies (which did visit Stratford-upon-Avon) and featuring usually an entertaining array of Deadly Sins and Vices. There is an amusing example – the Marriage of Wit and Wisdom – in the play *Sir Thomas More* of the 1590s.[2]

At grammar schools and university colleges, boys and young men would have studied Latin comedies and tragedies, which had been frequently republished in the Renaissance's revival of learning. The comedies of the Roman playwright

Plautus (3rd–2nd century BC) are the formal basis of farce-plots, featuring lovers who can't be united because of parental opposition, servants both quick-witted and dull who assist (or complicate) their cause, financial crises and scams, disguise and mistaken identities, and a last-minute resolution. They also contained a good deal of word-play, typically between master and servant. In the sixteenth century, these plays not only featured as the lighter aspect of a boy's classical education, they also mutated into the world of popular theatre – the strolling troupes of actors, jugglers, jesters, and musicians of whom we see an affectionate memorial in *Hamlet*'s Players.

The most famous professional troupes of strolling players were the Italian *Commedia dell'arte* companies. Commedia dell'arte is a distant derivative of Roman comedy that characteristically relies on improvisation – both verbal and physical – around the basic plot or scenario. We know that troupes of Italian commedia players and 'tumblers' visited England in the 1570–80s.[3] We can't say if Shakespeare saw them (or, indeed, if he perhaps visited Italy in the 1580s and saw them there). But since improvisation was a major skill of the professional clown in Elizabethan theatre, it seems likely that any new visual gags from the Italian players would have been quickly copied and adapted; and similarly that any *scenario* that had a potential for fast, largely physical comedy, would be picked up and exploited by troupes of travelling English players. Of course, the Italian companies – even those visiting England – used adult women in female roles, much scandalising the English who had a long tradition of considering any woman who performed in public to be a whore. The commedia companies also used adult men in drag for comic effect in roles such as nurses or brothel-keepers, a practice that was probably imitated on occasion in Shakespeare's theatre.

The Comedy of Errors

This early play (admired by Francis Meres; see ch. 1) demonstrates that Shakespeare knew his school classics and could adapt them – characteristically in a way that shows the young playwright's daring dramaturgical skills and his eclectic imagination. Shakespeare uses, from his source in the Roman playwright Plautus' plays, the unities of place (the street in Ephesus), time (from morning till 5pm of one day), and action (a single plot logically developed from one situation). Farce still tends to use these conventions (they are familiar from TV sitcoms), complete with mistaken identities, locked-door gags, etc. To Plautus' original play *The Menaechmi* with its twin brother protagonists – Antipholus of Syracuse, the visitor, and Antipholus of Ephesus, the local – he adds twin servants, the two Dromios, from another Plautus play, *Amphitruo*. The potential for visual jokes, mistaken identities, and double-takes as people appear from the 'wrong' part of the stage, is doubled. And so is the potential for laughter and pain. Violence is endemic in this play, and it somehow has to be negotiated so as to produce the illusion that any pain suffered from the infliction of violence is minimal, and disappears as quickly as the characters move on to the next unfolding of the plot – exactly like a child's game of cowboys and Indians: you're 'dead' while you count to twenty. It's *play*. This illusion can be created by self-conscious theatricality in both sets of twins' performances, and by confident, fast-paced acting that doesn't let the audience pause to question the irrational premises of the play.

The Comedy of Errors has an overplus of comic violence. Virtually every time one of the Dromios encounters either of the Antipholi, he is beaten. Adriana too (a typically shrewish, nagging wife straight out of Plautus) routinely beats Ephesian Dromio. This fact is punningly built into his normal discourse (his way of thinking about himself):

> I have some marks of yours upon my pate,
> Some of my mistress' marks upon my shoulders,
> But not a thousand marks [of money] between you both.
>
> (1.2.82–4)

Talking in a comic way about being beaten defuses the reality, because it demonstrates to the audience that it doesn't hurt sufficiently to deprive the clowns of their wit:[4]

> DROMIO OF EPHESUS ... I have served him from the hour of my nativity to this instant, and have nothing at his hands for my service but blows. When I am cold, he heats me with beating; when I am warm, he cools me with beating. I am waked with it when I sleep, raised with it when I sit, driven out of doors with it when I go from home, welcomed home with it when I return.   (4.4.27–33)

> DROMIO OF SYRACUSE Was there ever any man thus beaten out of season,
> When in the why and the wherefore is neither rhyme nor reason?
>
> (2.2.46–7)

Productions will often use a barrage of percussion sound effects for every comic blow suffered by the Dromios, including being hit with metal trays (cymbals), or 'clocked' on the head with various objects. Drums and whistles can be on hand to underline various other moments of physical comedy. This is a technique also used in early films and vaudeville (for example in the work of Buster

Keaton, early Chaplin, Laurel and Hardy, the Marx Brothers) – and we will see it consciously used again in *The Taming of the Shrew* (the 'Knock me here' joke of 1.2). Another farce technique that was taken up by early cinema, and that we can enjoy as *The Comedy of Errors* approaches its climax, is the 'Keystone Cops' chase through the streets and marketplace, involving almost all the cast (end of Act 4 – note the Folio stage direction: 'Exeunt omnes as fast as may be, frighted.'). 'I see these witches are afraid of swords', says Syracusan Antipholus, often at this point brandishing some quite inadequate comedy sword (umbrella, toy from market stall, stick of rhubarb). The attempted 'exorcism' of Antipholus of Ephesus by the 'conjuror' Dr Pinch, obviously a charlatan, offers another opportunity for elaborate visual gags, one that is nicely rounded off when Pinch is reportedly beaten, singed, and soused with 'puddled mire' by the irate Antipholus (who, being a local, had probably been wanting to do this for a while to the con-man). Often the bedraggled Pinch will be paraded on stage at this point – but this real physical harm is not put on stage by Shakespeare: there is no stage direction for Pinch's re-entry (contrast Malvolio's bitter re-entry in the last scene of *Twelfth Night*). No doubt the audience, however, is always happy to see his humiliation.

This episode of the conjuror, Dr Pinch, developed by Shakespeare from the Plautine story's Doctor, provides an entry-point into the unique aspects of the play, that is, what Shakespeare did with his source material to turn it into a play that transcends farce, or at the very least, re-contextualises it. The two key words are magic and time. If the effectiveness of farce depends on a fast pace and split-second comic timing by the actors, that's one thing. But if you add to this the possibility that the world the visitors have stumbled into 'is the fairy land', as Dromio says to the audience –

> We talk with goblins, ouphs [elves' children], and sprites.
> If we obey them not, this will ensue:
> They'll suck our breath, or pinch us black and blue.
>
> (2.2.181–3)

– then everything they see and experience is not just confusing but profoundly disorienting (this of course is how modern conjurors get their effects). Even the bourgeois wife Adriana, as the play reaches its climax of absurdity, says that her husband is

> borne about invisible:
> Even now we hous'd him in the abbey *here*,
> And now he's *there*, past thought of human reason.
>
> (5.1.187–9; italics added)

There's a real sense that the characters have found themselves not just in Ephesus (though that was biblically famous for sorcery) but in something like the wood outside Athens of *A Midsummer Night's Dream* that Shakespeare had yet to conjure from his imagination. 'Reason' does not seem to operate here:

> DROMIO OF SYRACUSE No, no, the bell. 'Tis time that I were gone,
> It was two ere I left him, and now the clock strikes one.
> ADRIANA The hours come back; that did I never hear.   (4.2.53–5)

All the major characters obsess about time, and its basic, ordering relation to 'reason' or 'season'. When that is upset, then the world is topsy-turvy, and anything might happen – a person appear in two places at once, for example – by magic or sorcery.

But for one character in the play, time's inexorable and reasonable progress is terrifying, indeed life-threatening: Egeon, the father of the Antipholi. A fascinating example of Shakespeare's dramatic instincts is that Egeon and his dilemma literally frame the play – he only appears at its beginning and end; if he has not raised the large fine demanded of him by the end of the day he will die by the Duke's decree. So, issues of life and death (and money) as they are normally lived (i.e. by the audience) are signalled firmly as the 'play' itself allows us two hours time out, two hours of simple laughter at the complications caused by mistaken identity, two hours in which cruelty to servants or marital infidelity, for example, is unproblematic, before returning the world to normal reality. And the key aspect of 'normality' is relationships, principally those of the family (with romance, if it happens, as a bonus).

Here Shakespeare, the true magician, pulls another rabbit out of the hat: the moment when both sets of twins see each other for the first time. It's what the audience has been waiting for and expecting – so the basic dramatic value of suspense is invoked – but it is much more than that. It is in fact magic – the magic of stagecraft, in which two sets of actors, and their costume and make-up designers, have used all their technique to convince us that they are identical. (Productions where one actor plays both Dromios, with a double coming on only at the end, can be somewhat unsatisfying: they can give too much power to one 'star' comedy actor rather than to the text and the ensemble performance.) The writing for both sets of twins goes far beyond the simple comic resolution of the farcical errors: Shakespeare calls up some profoundly beautiful poetry to move as well as delight us with the mystery of human identity and the strange but strong bonds of familial relationships. This note was struck briefly in the play's opening:

ANTIPHOLUS OF SYRACUSE He that commends me to mine
    own content
Commends me to the thing I cannot get.
I to the world am like a drop of water
That in the ocean seeks another drop,
Who, falling there to find his fellow forth,
Unseen, inquisitive, confounds himself.
So I, to find a mother and a brother,
In quest of them unhappy, lose myself.   (1.2. 33–40)

The wandering Antipholus of Syracuse, the more spiritual and sentimental
brother, most doubts his identity throughout the play, and his experiences evoke
(albeit comically) the questing hero of ancient myth. His brother, Antipholus
of Ephesus, is the embodiment of physical life – sex, food, and money are most
important to him, settled as he is in a mercantile town. Together, as Syracusan
Antipholus foreshadows in this early speech, they make up the image of a whole
human being. (So of course he will marry Adriana's sister at the play's end.)
As for the Dromio twins, there is little sense of differentiation: they are both
basically physical bodies (although Dromio of Syracuse has clearly learnt wit in
the service of his master – witness their comedy routines: the quick exchange
of riddles on 'time' in 2.2; the virtuoso riff on the 'geography' of Nell the
kitchenmaid in 3.2). As servants, however, they are genuinely indistinguishable
to their masters and mistresses. Out of this brutally realistic class perception
springs the egalitarian poetry that ends the play with a poignant final physical
image. It is a 'built-in' stage direction:

DROMIO OF EPHESUS Methinks you are my glass, and not my
    brother.
I see by you I am a sweet-faced youth.
Will you walk in to see their gossiping?
DROMIO OF SYRACUSE Not I, sir. You are my elder.
DROMIO OF EPHESUS That's a question. How shall we try it?
DROMIO OF SYRACUSE We'll draw cuts for the senior. Till then, lead
    thou first.
DROMIO OF EPHESUS Nay then, thus:
We came into the world like brother and brother,
And now let's go hand in hand, not one before another.   (5.1.417–25)

The Comedy of Errors both *is* classical farce and transcends it, its final image
offering the two clowns as embodiments of the physical 'magic' of the theatre
and the stories it can tell us about identity, society, and family.

The Taming of the Shrew

The Taming of the Shrew, dating from about 1594, presents a large-scale naturalisation of commedia dell'arte character types and plot. It also draws on native English popular drama, in particular for its dealings with the 'shrewish' woman. There is a long tradition in English theatre and in popular ballads and tracts[5] that criticises the talkative, hot-tempered, and ungovernable woman: she can be seen, for example, in Noah's wife in the Mystery plays (she refuses to come into the Ark, preferring to sit and gossip with her women friends); or, later, in Judy in the Punch and Judy puppet show (which arrived in England from Italy in the seventeenth century); as well as in Plautus (as represented by Adriana in *The Comedy of Errors*). The solution to the shrew's perceived misbehaviour is almost always physical force on the part of her husband – that is, he can't subjugate her by 'reason', since women are traditionally irrational in medieval gender ideology (they are principally bodies, not minds; some theologians even doubted if women had souls). But in commedia dell'arte and its ancestor Roman comedy, blustering authority figures – fathers, husbands, doctors, soldiers – don't always win unequivocally.

Commedia and comedy

We can map the major characters of *The Taming of the Shrew* onto the commedia model – with the possible exception of Katherina, the 'shrew' herself, whose characterisation I will discuss separately.

Petruchio is the Cavaliere: a suave womaniser, a man who believes in his ability to charm any woman. Like many such figures, he is also in need of money, and so seeks to settle down in marriage – 'I come to wive it wealthily in Padua; / If wealthily, then happily in Padua,' he declares (1.2.72–3). His first encounter with Katherina (2.1, discussed below) shows him that he will need more than his fabled charm: he will need to theatrically exaggerate the 'wooing' situation in order to disorient Kate from her rusted-on misanthropic attitude. His fantastical outfit at the wedding, and his behaviour thereafter, is a deliberately theatrical performance of the commedia's Capitano, a blustering, bullying military man who will only temporarily have the upper hand. In 3.2 the audience is helped by Biondello's over-the-top description to see this cartoonish figure as one of broken-down masculinity:

> Why, Petruchio is coming in a new hat and an old jerkin; a pair of old
> breeches thrice turned; a pair of boots that have been candle-cases, one
> buckled, another laced; an old rusty sword tane out of the town
> armoury, with a broken hilt and chapeless; [etc.]   (3.2.41–4)

Katherina's father, Baptista, is the classic Pantalone figure: old, moneyed, a powerful patriarch in a family that has no mother. He wants to marry off his daughters – Bianca, possibly, to his old friend Gremio, who is labelled 'a pantaloon' at his first entry (stage direction 1.1.45) – but he is easily tricked by the more energetic and resourceful young people. The lovers, Bianca and Lucentio, are commedia's typically clever and wilful girl and her lover, assisted by his servants; they eventually, through disguise and trickery, get exactly what they want, in both love and fortune.

The servants, known as *zanni* in commedia, provide most of the visual gags as well as assisting in the plot (if they're of the clever Brighella type, like Tranio) or endangering it (if they're of the dimmer Arlecchino type: Biondello comes close to this,[6] but he has a useful role to play in his naively astonished reporting of Petruchio's wedding outfit, as we saw above). Commedia depended for most of its comic effects on gags, known as *lazzi*, largely surplus to the plot. These were often quite extended improvisational passages, with extravagant physical byplay. Shakespeare has scripted several. For example, early in the play (1.2), as Petruchio and his man Grumio arrive in Padua, there is the classic 'Knock me here' gag, which depends upon Grumio not understanding a clear instruction he must, realistically, have heard a thousand times before:

> PETRUCHIO ... Here, sirrah Grumio, knock, I say.
> GRUMIO Knock, sir? Whom should I knock? Is there any man has
>   rebused your worship?
> PETRUCHIO Villain, I say, knock me here soundly.
> GRUMIO Knock you here, sir? Why, sir, what am I, sir, that I should
>   knock you here, sir? [etc.]   (1.2.5–10)

The upshot is the stage direction, 'He wrings him by the ears' – once again the servant is physically abused. This somewhat tired gag does in fact have thematic relevance. Katherina's introduction into the play matches Petruchio for potential violence: in 2.1 she comes on stage pulling her sister, whose hands she has bound, and she then chases her off with threats of more abuse. In Petruchio and Katherina's first meeting, there is actual violence from Kate ('She strikes him', stage direction at 2.1.214), and he holds her down ('Why does the world report that Kate doth limp?' as she struggles to escape). Actors and directors have to choose how comically these scenes are performed: the proximity of farcical beating to the experience of actual pain and humiliation is the more evident once 'gentlefolk' of both genders begin to indulge in it between themselves.

We are later told by the shocked Gremio that Petruchio has continued his violent and ungenteel behaviour in the church:

> I'll tell you, Sir Lucentio: when the priest
> Should ask if Katherine should be his wife,
> 'Ay, by gogs-wouns!' quoth he, and swore so loud
> That, all-amazed, the priest let fall the book;
> And as he stooped again to take it up,
> This mad-brained bridegroom took him such a cuff
> That down fell priest and book, and book and priest!
> 'Now take them up,' quoth he, 'if any list.'
>
> (3.2.148–55)

This is edgy, because it is sacrilegious misbehaviour in a church: the Elizabethan audience probably wouldn't be comfortable *seeing* this, but they were perhaps rather guiltily enthralled to *hear* about it. Does it, however, imply that Petruchio is going too far, that this conscious performance of hyper-masculinity suggests its moral limitations? It is at the end of this scene that Petruchio spells out the brutal realities of patriarchal ideology:

> I will be master of what is mine own.
> She is my goods, my chattels; she is my house,
> My household-stuff, my field, my barn,
> My horse, my ox, my ass, my anything,
> And here she stands. Touch her whoever dare,
> I'll bring mine action on the proudest he
> That stops my way in Padua.   (3.2.218–24)

The traditional 'comic business' at this point is that Petruchio slings Katherina over his shoulder and exits with her. It's a conclusion that, once again, raises the issue of whether farce violence is funny if you are actually on the receiving end of it.

Act 4's arrival at Petruchio's house brings on stage the physical 'taming' of this 'chattel', Katherina. It is difficult, certainly in today's world, to keep this physical comedy within the light-hearted conventions of farce. Servants are bullied and struck as Kate watches; food is thrown about the stage as she is denied it; Petruchio takes her to the bridal chamber only to throw the bedding round the room and refuse to let her sleep. The following day Petruchio destroys before her (and our) eyes the new clothes he had ordered for her.[7] The play *can* work today – but perhaps not as farce.

The wooing

Can it work as romantic comedy? That is, is it possible for a charismatic pair of actors playing Katherina and Petruchio to overcome the obstacles that the 'taming' plot puts in their way and convince us that they are really in love, and only need to work out a *modus vivendi*? Shakespeare was working increasingly in the 1590s on the comic potential of young lovers – both those who believed whole-heartedly in the literary conventions of Petrarchan love as models for courtship (see chapters 3, 4 and 5), and those who were sceptical about any ideology that would force them to modify their behaviour. The latter type appear throughout his work – and arguably, Kate and Petruchio are such a couple.

The clue is in their verbal exchanges, not their rough-housing, which relates too disturbingly to the Punch and Judy model. Act 2 scene 1 offers the audience 90 lines in which they are alone on stage, testing their wits against each other (as Beatrice and Benedick will do, in shorter bursts, four or five years later). They are clearly evenly matched – though Petruchio has more words, reflecting his dominant social position. Kate's barbed comments respond tellingly to Petruchio's sarcasm and double-entendres. It would be unbelievable if at this early point they were seen to 'fall in love' – Katherina has still too much anger within herself about the whole patriarchal system, as the end of the scene makes clear; but there is nothing against their recognising a sense of physical attraction, even if reluctantly, in Kate's case. The play's first 'Kiss me, Kate' occurs as they exit – Petruchio 'to Venice', Katherina further into her father's house. Whether they kiss – and whether it is forced or mutually enjoyable – will set the tone for their next encounter. This is at the wedding; and it is obvious from Katherina's speeches both before and after the event that she has been in some way moved by being wooed by Petruchio. She feels the shame of possible rejection:

> I must, forsooth, be forced
> To give my hand, opposed against my heart,
> Unto a mad-brain rudesby, full of spleen,
> Who wooed in haste and means to wed at leisure.
> I told you, I, he was a frantic fool,
> Hiding his bitter jests in blunt behaviour.
> . . . Now must the world point at poor Katherine,
> And say, 'Lo, there is mad Petruchio's wife
> If it would please him come and marry her!'
>
> (3.2.8–13, 18–20)

After the unconventional wedding (as described by Gremio) Katherina seems momentarily hopeful of a new life, 'entreating' her husband 'if you love me, stay' (3.2.194); but Petruchio calls for his horse, and carries off his new wife, whose last words are, ominously, 'I see a woman may be made a fool / If she had not a spirit to resist' (3.2.209–10). This moment presages the unpleasant spectacle of Katherina's various humiliations in Act 4, all according to Petruchio's plan: 'Thus have I politicly begun my reign . . . And thus I'll curb her mad and headstrong humour', he tells the audience. There is no aspiration towards mutuality here. Kate has no equivalent soliloquy. She makes one attempt to claim autonomy, to return to the shared intellectual ground of their first meeting –

> Why, sir, I trust I may have leave to speak,
> And speak I will. I am no child, no babe.
> Your betters have endured me say my mind,
> And if you cannot, best you stop your ears.
> My tongue will tell the anger of my heart,
> Or else my heart concealing it will break,
> And, rather than it shall, I will be free
> Even to the uttermost, as I please, in words.
> (4.3.73–80)

Insultingly, Petruchio ignores this plea for respect and hearing; he continues to address her simply as a clothes mannequin.

Petruchio's 'taming' policy – nothing less than bullying (though he never hits her) – reduces Katherina to the lowest in the household hierarchy. Although he beats the servants, at least they eat; Kate is deprived of food. Many actresses, desperate for a romantic ending, argue that in the 'sun and moon' scene (4.6) Kate learns to play Petruchio's game – even treating it as an erotic game. However, this scene can be performed in many ways: submissively, sullenly, flirtatiously, ironically. All we have is her words of capitulation:

> sun it is not, when you say it is not,
> And the moon changes even as your mind.
> What you will have it named, even that it is,
> And so it shall be so for Katherine.
> (4.5.19–22)

'Petruchio, go thy ways, the field is won' comments Hortensio (a wishful thinker?). Better evidence for a romantic ending might be found in the one mutually agreed kiss that occurs at the end of 5.1. Even that, however, is according to Petruchio's plan, and can be played with different nuances. He insists on her kissing him in public, a somewhat indecorous show of affection or desire, and when she gives in, he concludes triumphantly, 'Is not this well? Come, my sweet Kate, / Better once than never, for never too late' (5.1.124–5).

This is where, probably, a genuine romantic comedy would end. But Shakespeare adds the extraordinary last scene, in which Katherina is asked to publicly demonstrate her 'taming'. There's a final reminder of her humiliation: she takes off her new cap and throws it underfoot when Petruchio commands her to. Then there is her speech of instruction to those women who remain 'shrews':

> Fie, fie, unknit that threatening unkind brow,
> And dart not scornful glances from those eyes
> To wound thy lord, thy king, thy governor.
>
> (5.2.136–8)

There are 44 lines of it, justifying the patriarchy, arguing that it is the best guarantee of marital happiness, and ending with a strong visual image of submission, a built-in stage direction:

> Then vail your stomachs, for it is no boot,
> And place your hands below your husband's foot.
> In token of which duty, if he please,
> My hand is ready, may it do him ease.
>
> (5.2.175–9)

Some Katherinas speak this with heavy irony, some with a sort of brainwashed fervour. The real question here is, what does Petruchio do as she speaks? Since at least 1978[8] he has usually looked embarrassed at what he's forced her to spell out; his 'Kiss me, Kate' at the end of it must be one of the most difficult lines for a modern actor in all comedy (matched perhaps only by Valentine's giving away his girlfriend to his best friend who has just tried to rape her in *Two Gentlemen*; see chapter 3). There is a final piece of business as Petruchio reminds Lucentio that he has 'won the wager', and presumably collects his money. With what demeanour does he do this, and how does Kate react to see herself and her new marriage the subject of a bar-room gamble?

The frame

All these questions are built into the play's dramaturgy, so that the audience is (at least unconsciously) challenged, via a confrontation with the limits of farce and its tendency to cruelty and violence. We are prompted to see the story in this perspective by the fact that the play has a 'frame'– if directors choose to use it. As published (in both its versions, Quarto and Folio), the *Taming* play begins with what is called an Induction, which has several scenes: a fantasy at some removes from the realities of contemporary Elizabethan life. Christopher Sly the drunken tinker – a type who would be recognised by the audience as a realistic local figure, making a nuisance of himself at the pub – becomes subject to an episode of cultural and class bullying by the anonymous Lord and his huntsmen. They are much more 'literary' figures; they speak blank verse and seem to come from the world of medieval romance and high culture:

> LORD O monstrous beast, how like a swine he lies!
> Grim death, how foul and loathsome is thine image!
> Sirs, I will practise on this drunken man.
> What think you, if he were conveyed to bed,
> Wrapped in sweet clothes, rings put upon his fingers,
> A most delicious banquet by his bed,
> And brave attendants near him when he wakes –
> Would not the beggar then forget himself?
>
> (Induction 1.30–7)

The Lord convinces Sly that he (Sly, who momentarily also finds himself able to speak in blank verse) is an aristocrat who has recovered from a long bout of lunacy. Players fortuitously arrive and are also brought unwittingly into the trick. The Lord has also dragooned his young page Bartholomew into playing Sly's aristocratic 'wife': he is given instructions about how to perform this role, including putting an onion in his handkerchief to induce tears at appropriate moments. There are many passages in the Induction that alert the audience to the artificiality of theatre – that is, in particular, to the *Taming* play which is to come – but perhaps the most striking one is the dialogue that closes the Induction, when Sly asks about the genre of the play to be performed:

> SLY Is not a comonty a Christmas gambold, or a tumbling-trick?
> BARTHOLOMEW No, my good lord, it is more pleasing stuff.
> SLY What, household stuff?
> BARTHOLOMEW It is a kind of history.   (Induction 2.132–6)

Comedy is 'history', that is, not as the doings of kings and princes, but as a 'story' that tells middle-class folk about themselves – though, like all history, always selectively and from a particular perspective. If the *Taming* is played as Sly's fantasy of masculine domination (the roles of Sly and Petruchio are often doubled in modern productions), the audience is all the more encouraged to see it as amusing, but the frame cuts it off from reference to their own lives. The frame is unfinished at the end of Shakespeare's play in the 1623 Folio text, making the play even more disconcertingly open and incomplete.[9] That is, it throws the issues of the relevance of the 'history' back onto the actors and the audience, for them to make local sense of. What we have in *The Taming of the Shrew* is, arguably, a young playwright looking at the traditions and sources of contemporary comedy and deciding that he can take it further – turning a classic farce, where artificial chaos is finally resolved in a simple solution, into something far more unstable that relates in uncomfortable ways to the structures underlying the real life of the Elizabethan audience.

The Merry Wives of Windsor

Only one of Shakespeare's comedies has a local 'real world' setting – not in London, where other playwrights set their 'city comedies', but in the royal town of Windsor. Contemporary mores concerning class and courtship are very much to the fore in this late farce of 1597, called, significantly, *The **Merry Wives** of Windsor*.

Mistress Page is one of two well-married and prosperous housewives. When she receives a letter proposing an assignation from the fat and ageing knight Sir John Falstaff, she is outraged and eloquent:

> What an unweighed behaviour hath this Flemish drunkard picked –
> with the devil's name – out of my conversation, that he dares in this
> manner assay me? Why, he hath not been thrice in my company. What
> should I say to him? I was then frugal of my mirth. Heaven forgive me!
> Why, I'll exhibit a bill in the parliament for the putting down of men.
> How shall I be revenged on him? For revenged I will be, as sure as his
> guts are made of puddings.   (2.1.19–25)

This sentiment is shared by her friend, Mistress Ford, who arrives with an identical letter: 'What tempest, I trow, threw this whale, with so many tuns of oil in his belly, ashore at Windsor? How shall I be revenged on him?' (2.1.50–1). Might the Elizabethan audience be hearing something that they could identify as Katherina's revenge? Or the triumph of English bourgeois good sense over older misogynistic myths? Mistress Ford, it emerges, is subject to her husband's irrational jealousy – she has more than one reason to desire that men be taught a lesson (and something more practical than 'a bill in the parliament', Mistress Page's utopian solution).

Mistress Ford goes on to point out that Falstaff is not only a drunk and a glutton, he is also a lecher. There is an assumption that the audience will share the perspective voiced by the 'normal' housewife, that Sir John Falstaff is a character who deserves his comeuppance. From the perspective of the tradition of native English drama, that is, Falstaff can be seen as playing a role carried over from the morality plays – he represents at least two of the seven deadly sins, gluttony and lechery. He is also a literal embodiment of farce, a 'stuffed' man.

Kaiser Falstaff

If Falstaff is the comedy fat man who can get a laugh just by walking on stage, he also embodies in his substantial person two other major dramatic traditions. He is the braggart soldier (Capitano) of commedia dell'arte, always claiming to be braver, cleverer, and more attractive than any other man – and always being proved wrong. Most interesting, perhaps, is that in the English tradition, he can be seen as a version of the Vice – the character in morality plays who wittily and often outrageously appeals to our urge to 'get away with' sinning.

Shakespeare's fat knight appears in three plays of the 1590s – *Henry IV Parts I* and *II*, and *The Merry Wives of Windsor*. (His death is reported, poignantly, in an early scene of *Henry V*.) A story which can be traced to no earlier than 1702 reports that *The Merry Wives* was written at the command of Queen Elizabeth, who wished to see 'Sir John in love'. Certainly the curious fact that this is the only one of Shakespeare's plays set in a recognisably contemporary Elizabethan England suggests something special about its composition. The comedy, however, enacts the humiliation of the fat knight: might Shakespeare have guessed that such a story would be particularly pleasing to the imperious Elizabeth, who tolerated no presumptions of love or power from her male favourites? Elizabeth herself, one of whose royal residences was at Windsor, might be symbolised in the cunning actions of the Merry Wives – female 'politicians' – who control the plot of the comedy. Comedy, we recall, works towards a vision of regeneration in the community, the expulsion of anti-social forces; it celebrates the community's ability to resolve its problems without the violence of revolution. This was an issue of some relevance in the 1590s, as the question of the ageing Queen's successor became urgent.

In the last scene of *The Merry Wives* Falstaff disguises himself as Herne the Hunter in order, as he thinks, to fulfil his fantasy of seduction. The disguise, which he evidently relishes for the stag-horn headdress which (to him) signifies male sexual power, is in fact dictated by the Wives with their different agenda – and might more accurately be read as 'the horns', the sign of sexual defeat. Falstaff is teased and pinched out of his lecherous folly by a band of children, performing as 'fairies' under the Wives' direction – the women and children of the community working together to drive out the disruptive and anarchic force of unbridled lust and greed. It is important for the audience to see that conversion is brought about *not* by the supernatural actions of real fairies (as in *A Midsummer Night's Dream*) but by ordinary village children dressing-up and tapping into the power of folk-myth. Children are a sign of the community's vitality, its continuity centred on the family; and this comedy values the sexual impulse for the relations it creates, most particularly those of a young man and a young woman, leading to marriage and the production of more children. Irresponsible lechery such as Falstaff's – and his belief that every woman, married or not, is just waiting for his attentions – is destructive of this larger picture. And social and financial marriages (such as that proposed by the middle-aged Dr Caius for Anne) are a poor second-best to a marriage based on romantic love that assumes mutually enjoyable sexual activity in a well-matched couple. As her lover Fenton says to Anne's father in his last and most eloquent speech in the play, 'You would have married her, most shamefully, / Where there was no proportion held in love' (5.5.191–2).

The lust of old men like Falstaff and Caius is inappropriate; it has only its own gratification as a goal. From this perspective they are Pantalone and *il Dottore* of commedia dell'arte – both men are equally interested in the money their desired matches will bring. But further, Falstaff is an English Lord of Misrule, eating, drinking, and wenching his way through life with a gargantuan appetite. Out of place in a respectable small-town community, he is more at home in the taverns of London's Eastcheap (in the *Henry IV* plays) or on the battlefield, faking death and glory – that is, playing the somewhat less complex comedy roles of Braggart and Vice in an exclusively male community. What is lacking in those earlier environments in which Falstaff first appeared is the wives and mothers, the children and marriageable girls, who provide an alternative ethic to the world of egoistic competition and 'honour' that the men inhabit. Ford's groundless jealousy, the duel between Dr Caius and the Welsh parson, Bardolph's and Pistol's attempts to keep up a soldierly image despite the parasitic reality of their lives, are all summed up in the mighty figure of Falstaff. Falstaff literally towers over the other men of the play – as the Host says, 'Thou'rt an emperor: Caesar, Kaiser, and Pheasar'[10] (1.3.6) – and he thereby represents a cartoonish masculinity in the play's symbolic argument of the bullies versus the unstoppably talkative wives.

A community such as that of Windsor is nominally and legally a patriarchy, but the play demonstrates that the married women have a more realistic grasp of what is actually going on in their small world. This knowledge is spread through female gossip and friendship – Mistress Page and Mistress Ford share their ludicrous proposals from Falstaff, rather than keeping them to themselves in the hope of personal advantage. Their acts of 'revenge' on this overweening masculine figure are all based on their traditional feminine roles, their areas of domestic expertise. The dirty linen of the washing-basket trick is 'women's business': it is a sweet revenge to treat the fat knight as no more than the soiled shirts or tablecloths that his gluttonous lifestyle creates.[11]

The emphasis on the domestic setting of the play actually enables scenes that are close to the modern notion of farce as manic activity that explodes in a confined space – bedroom or living-room. Falstaff's uncomfortable sojourn in the washing-basket – and from thence in the river – offers glorious opportunities for clothes to be flung about the stage, actors jumping on the basket to squash down the fat man, and comic attempts to heave the weighty basket up and get it out of the room as the wasp-like Ford and his caricatured colleagues rage ineffectively.

Falstaff, still deluded, returns to his project of seduction; and his next forced escape involves him being dressed up as the 'fat woman of Brentford', a woman so ugly that she is an object of repulsion rather than desire. Falstaff is made to feel literally what it is like to be a woman, one without even the power of sexual allure: Ford beats 'her' out of the house as a witch. From self-appointed hero and 'Kaiser' to grotesque female body: it is a comprehensive humiliation.

But even after this Falstaff is unable to comprehend that the invitation to meet Alice Ford at midnight at Herne's Oak is anything other than a compliment to his irresistible virility: as he waits for her he likens himself to lustful Jove, playing out the grand sexual myths of Western culture. The audience, however, hears a descent from poetic soliloquy to a solo riff from a comic actor who knows himself to be at base simply a fat man:

> Now, the hot-blooded gods assist me! Remember, Jove, thou wast a bull for thy Europa. Love set on thy horns. O powerful love, that in some respects makes a beast a man, in some other a man a beast! You were also, Jupiter, a swan for the love of Leda. O omnipotent love, how near the god drew to the complexion of a goose! . . . For me, I am here a Windsor stag, and the fattest, I think, i'th'forest. Send me a cool rut-time, Jove, or who can blame me to piss my tallow?   (5.5.2–11)

Within minutes he is lying on the ground, terrified lest he sets eyes on the 'fairies'. Keen theatre-goers might be reminded at this point of his 'playing dead' on the battlefield in *1 Henry IV* (5.4); this is typical behaviour for the braggart soldier of comedy. Here, in the 'women's revenge' play, for the third time his huge body is belaboured and his dignity pricked like a balloon.

Given this comprehensive humiliation, why has Falstaff remained such a well-loved comic figure? Generally, the fat knight's popularity is the effect of his rather more complex role in the *Henry* plays, where he represents a critique of the deadly traditions of the court and a life-enhancing father-figure for young Hal; in the battlefield scene his survival tactic actually earns the audience's admiration. But further, the fat-bellied Lord of Misrule, whether as Bacchus or Falstaff or Santa Claus, is a guarantee that the community has an abundance of good things, such that on occasion it can allow excess and self-indulgence the opportunity to play, before returning to the sober realities of everyday life. In this sense Falstaff represents the greedy child in all of us, with an almost indestructible self-esteem and an uncomplicated taste for bodily pleasures. And this relates Falstaff to another comic archetype: the Clown.

All Shakespeare's clowns have a turn for linguistic invention, and an ability to contest any situation with a fusillade of words. Falstaff, being technically the highest-status person in the play (a knight of the realm), acts on the belief that he has the right to take what he wants. But he talks about this impulse in ways that create a warm empathy with the audience, and laughter, as in the example quoted above. His metaphors indicate a sense of the prosperity of the world that he and his audience inhabit:

> O, she did so course o'er my exteriors, with such a greedy intention, that
> the appetite of her eye did seem to scorch me up like a burning-glass . . .
> She is a region in Guiana, all gold and bounty. I will be cheaters to
> them both, and they shall be exchequers to me. They shall be my East
> and West Indies, and I will trade to them both.   (1.3.48–53)

In love, Falstaff cries, 'Let the sky rain potatoes, let it thunder to the tune of "Greensleeves", hail kissing-comfits, and snow eryngoes' (5.5.14–16; 'eryngoes' are Elizabethan candies with an aphrodisiac reputation). Almost his last line in the play is ''Tis time I were choked with a piece of toasted cheese.' All that food has to produce an energy that in some sense vitalises the community, however waywardly. Falstaff is not destroyed and cast out at the end of the comedy, he is invited to go home to the Pages' house, to 'laugh this sport o'er by a country fire; Sir John and all'. It is perhaps the least ambivalent ending of any of the comedies: the anarchy of farce, driven by men's desires, is comfortably brought into domestic harmony, under the control of the '*merry* wives'.[12]

Chapter 3

Courtly lovers and the real world

Courtly love

One of the most influential literary ideas in the medieval period was that of *amour courtois*, courtly love. It originated with the troubadours of southern France in the twelfth century, and its principal characteristics are these:

> the courtly lover idealizes his beloved; she, his sovereign lady, occupies an exalted position above him. His feelings for her ennoble him and make him more worthy; her beauty of body and soul makes him long for union with her, not for passion's sake but as a means of achieving the ultimate in moral excellence.[1]

The important thing to note is that this was not a particularly common (or sensible) way of actually behaving; it was an excuse for poetry. And very early in the development of the poetic fashion it began to morph into something considerably less idealistic: an emphasis on the physical beauties of the distant beloved (often as a *blazon*, an elaborately descriptive list), and on the physical sufferings of the frustrated lover (sighing, burning, lack of appetite, sleeplessness, etc.); 'ennoblement' began to disappear, possibly because it's a concept that is rather less amenable to visual metaphor. Complaints about the lady's cruelty took its place.

The fourteenth-century Italian poet Francesco Petrarca (Petrarch) wrote a superb collection of poems (*Canzoniere* or *Rime*) about his love for a lady called Laura. Influential throughout Europe, they were translated, adapted and imitated in the early sixteenth century in fine poems by Sir Thomas Wyatt and Henry Howard, Earl of Surrey. Sir Philip Sidney brought English Petrarchism to its greatest poetic utterance in his *Astrophil and Stella* (published in 1591 after his untimely death); and many other poets of the period followed the fashion of writing long sonnet sequences about the experience of being in love. This sonnet by Samuel Daniel is a typical example from his sequence *Delia* (1592):

> Fair is my Love and cruel as she's fair;
> Her brow-shades frown, although her eyes are sunny.
> Her smiles are lightning, though her pride despair,
> And her disdains are gall, her favours honey:
> A modest maid, deck'd with a blush of honour,
> Whose feet do tread green paths of youth and love;
> The wonder of all eyes that look upon her,
> Sacred on earth, design'd a Saint above.
> Chastity and Beauty, which were deadly foes,
> Live reconciled friends within her brow;
> And had she Pity to conjoin with those,
> Then who had heard the plaints I utter now?
> For had she not been fair, and thus unkind,
> My Muse had slept, and none had known my mind.

The appeal to the 'Muse' in the last line is the giveaway. This was a literary fashion, its main object being to show off the elegance and invention of the writer's style. Most of the writers were male, and it clearly suited them to have their beloved a silent and distant object, with no inner life of her own, so that the poet could perform (even posture) his agonies with great confidence – she would never speak or come down from her pedestal. Her voice is rarely or never heard in these poems; all we get is his myth of her, the way he wants her to be seen.

It should be noted that this was not the only form of fashionable love-poetry around at the time: even more popular was the pastoral, which often gave equal speech time to 'fair Phyllis' or 'Dorinda', in a witty dialogue of which the unspoken topic was a contest over the girl's virginity. Shakespeare plays with this model in *As You Like It* in the Rosalind/Orlando dialogues, while sending up the Petrarchan model in Orlando's own terrible poems. Indeed the conventional image of the courtly lover by the late sixteenth century in England was material for satire, particularly on the stage, where the poetic attitudes of the lover can be translated into a specifically eccentric physical appearance. Here are some examples from Shakespearean plays from the very end of the century.

ROSALIND There is a man haunts the forest that abuses our young
plants with carving 'Rosalind' on their barks; hangs odes upon

hawthorns and elegies on brambles; all, forsooth, defying the name of Rosalind. If I could meet that fancy-monger, I would give him some good counsel, for he seems to have the quotidian of love upon him.

ORLANDO I am he that is so love-shaked. I pray you tell me your remedy.

ROSALIND There is none of my uncle's marks upon you. He taught me how to know a man in love, in which cage of rushes I am sure you are not prisoner.

ORLANDO What were his marks?

ROSALIND A lean cheek, which you have not; a blue eye and sunken, which you have not; an unquestionable spirit, which you have not; a beard neglected, which you have not – but I pardon you for that, for, simply, your having in beard is a younger brother's revenue. Then your hose should be ungartered, your bonnet unbanded, your sleeve unbuttoned, your shoe untied, and everything about you demonstrating a careless desolation.   (*As You Like It* 3.3.301–18)

Orlando, although he is behaving with pardonable idiocy in celebrating his love for Rosalind, is *not* recognisable as the conventional lover (in fact, he is in rude good health, as we know from his victory in the wrestling scene). The audience, thus, has a more positive attitude to him than they might have to the conventional courtly lover, moping around.

A couple of years later on the same stage, Hamlet is pretending to be mad, for his own very good reasons:

OPHELIA My lord, as I was sewing in my closet,
Lord Hamlet with his doublet all unbraced,
No hat upon his head, his stockings fouled,
Ungartered and down-gyvèd to his ankle,
Pale as his shirt, his knees knocking each other,
And with a look so piteous in purport
As if he had been loosèd out of hell
To speak of horrors – he comes before me.
POLONIUS Mad for thy love?

(*Hamlet* 2.1.74–83)

Polonius has a conventional interpretation of Hamlet's behaviour – but he is an old man, a man who 'in his youth, suffered much for love' in the acceptable Petrarchan fashion. This behaviour is utilised as a strategy by the university-educated humanist Hamlet.

Two Gentlemen of Verona

Whereas by the end of the century such conventional behaviour by male lovers becomes a joke (Claudio in *Much Ado* laughs at the 'old signs' when Benedick succumbs (3.2.31)), in Shakespeare's early play *Two Gentlemen of Verona* (probably written 1590–1) a more carefully calibrated critique is made of the attitude to gender relations that underlies these 'Petrarchan' conventions. Valentine criticises Proteus, as the play begins, for his irrational subjection to love:

> VALENTINE To be in love: where scorn is bought with groans,
> Coy looks with heart-sore sighs, one fading moment's mirth
> With twenty watchful, weary, tedious nights;
> If haply won, perhaps a hapless gain;
> If lost, why then a grievous labour won;
> How ever, but a folly bought with wit,
> Or else a wit by folly vanquishèd.   (1.1.29–35)

But he too, before very long, will be behaving in a similarly irrational fashion, as he falls for Silvia (and she for him). Proteus, true to his name (= changer) and to the superficiality of his own attitude to love, also falls for Silvia as soon as Julia, his original beloved, is out of sight. These young men do not have a standard of adult behaviour from which their brief 'madness' of being in love deviates, as Benedick and Orlando do; as, indeed, even Hamlet does. For them, love is a constant madness and its female objects are largely indistinguishable. The play is quite blunt in displaying the callowness of the two young men: not only does Proteus change his love-object with aplomb, Valentine, supposedly the more mature of the two, at the climax of the play offers his beloved Silvia to Proteus as a sign of the value he puts on his friendship. Julia (disguised as a page and unrecognised by her 'master' Proteus) faints; Silvia says not another word to the end of the play.

The clowns

The young men's two servants, the clowns Speed and Lance, do not appear at all in the play's last act. Earlier, they have provided a satirical perspective on the behaviour of conventional lovers. When Valentine too falls in love, his servant Speed recites the signs by which this is evident:

> VALENTINE Why, how know you that I am in love?
> SPEED Marry, by these special marks: first, you have learned, like Sir
>   Proteus, to wreathe your arms like a malcontent; to relish a love-song

like a robin redbreast; to walk alone like one that had the pestilence; to sigh like a schoolboy that had lost his ABC; to weep like a young wench that had buried her grandam; to fast like one that takes diet; to watch like one that fears robbing; to speak puling like a beggar at Hallowmas. You were wont, when you laughed, to crow like a cock; when you walked, to walk like one of the lions; when you fasted, it was presently after dinner; when you looked sadly, it was for want of money. And now you are metamorphised with a mistress, that, when I look on you, I can hardly think you my master.   (2.1.15–27)

This perspective from a servant emphasises the cracks that had appeared in the structure of medieval aristocratic courtly love, under the sustained critique of Renaissance humanism. The subtext of Speed's observations is that this behaviour in one whom he calls master is simply irrational, and cannot be respected. When Lance tells us that he too is in love, it is in terms very different from the idealised self-regarding performance of his master: this nameless woman is valued because she is a milkmaid, a good brewer of ale, seamstress, knitter, spinner, and washerwoman – the perfect mistress of a working household. And if her breath is bad, if she's toothless, short-tempered, and not very bright, she is still a good marriage prospect, because she has some money (3.1).

The clowns speak for the people, a larger audience in the public theatres of late Elizabethan England than the aristocrats of court and great households. They also speak *to* the people, specifically the 'groundlings' who were closest to the stage in those theatres, and who paid a mere penny to stand, unprotected from the elements, but in a privileged position in regard to the characters on the stage. Whereas the male lovers (certainly not 'heroes') of *Two Gentlemen of Verona* cannot attract the audience's sympathy, the two clowns, Lance and Speed, are a pair of the finest comics that Shakespeare ever wrote. He gives them large amounts of stage time, together or separately, in conversation with their masters, and in asides and commentaries to the audience.

> VALENTINE Peace, here she comes.
> *Enter Silvia.*
> SPEED [*Aside*] O excellent motion! O exceeding puppet! Now will he interpret to her.
> VALENTINE Madam and mistress, a thousand good morrows.
> SPEED [*Aside*] O, 'give ye good even! Here's a million of manners.
> SILVIA Sir Valentine and servant, to you two thousand.
> SPEED [*Aside*] He should give her interest, and she gives it him.
>
> (2.1.81–8)

Running commentaries such as this on the behaviour of lovers set up a confidential relationship between the clown and the audience: we are amused, and even flattered, to see things from his satirical perspective rather than being sentimentally impressed by the lovers' overblown rhetoric.

Lance is the owner of a dog, Crab. Probably the clown in the company for whom Shakespeare wrote *Two Gentlemen* had had previous success in scenes with a dog; Shakespeare does not repeat this comic situation in later plays, despite its being a manifest audience-pleaser. Whatever size and type of dog is seen in this role, it is always funny simply because of the comments that dogs' natural movements make on the tale of woes that constitute Lance's utterance. Of course, a clever physical actor in a dog-suit can provide a different type of more knowing and inventive comic response (such as a dog might, if it could understand Shakespearean English). Lance and Crab have two scenes, 2.3 and 4.4. They are early examples of a scripted stand-up comedy monologue:

> LANCE Nay, 'twill be this hour ere I have done weeping; all the kind of the Lances have this very fault. I have received my proportion like the prodigious son and am going with Sir Proteus to the imperial's court. I think Crab, my dog, be the sourest-natured dog that lives: my mother weeping, my father wailing, my sister crying, our maid howling, our cat wringing her hands, and all our house in a great perplexity, yet did not this cruel-hearted cur shed one tear . . . Nay, I'll show you the manner of it. [*Taking off his shoes*] This shoe is my father. No, this left shoe is my father; no, no, this left shoe is my mother. Nay, that cannot be so neither. Yes, it is so, it is so: it hath the worser sole; this shoe with the hole in it is my mother – and this my father. A vengeance on't, there 'tis! Now, sir, this staff is my sister, for, look you, she is as white as a lily and as small as a wand. This hat is Nan, our maid. I am the dog. No, the dog is himself, and I am the dog. O, the dog is me, and I am myself. Ay, so, so. Now come I to my father; 'Father, your blessing.' Now should not the shoe speak a word for weeping . . . Now the dog all this while sheds not a tear nor speaks a word.   (2.3.1–27)

Very little linguistic alteration would be needed to make this monologue and its pair – the one about the dog farting in the grand banqueting-hall and peeing on a lady's dress (4.4) – into a routine at a modern comedy club. An absurdist imagination and an unstoppable linguistic associative flow are the essential tools of the stand-up monologist. If he can make the audience laugh, they are his friends. And an obliging dog (or even one that doesn't want to be there) is a brilliant prop.

There is a similar scripted clown scene in *The Merchant of Venice*, but it is touched with that play's darker themes. Lancelot has an equally funny monologue (without dog) on the question of whether he should leave 'this Jew my master' (2.2.1–24). He evokes the competing voices of Fiend and Conscience – comical shades of medieval morality plays – and when old Gobbo (Lancelot's father) arrives, a dim-witted straight man is added to the scene. But apart from this moment, Lancelot has not much opportunity to shine in the play: his role is subsumed into that of manservant and messenger, and opportunities for word-play and chat with the audience are limited. Any jokes he makes reflect the play's ideological concerns (as I describe them below); for example, commenting on Jessica's conversion to Christianity, 'This making of Christians will raise the price of hogs; if we grow all to be pork eaters, we shall not shortly have a rasher on the coals for money' (3.5.18–20). There is little room for absurdism in the tough world of the merchants of Venice.

The witty heroine

If stand-up comics have been, and still are, almost always male, what of the possibilities for comic women? Shakespeare experiments in this early play with a type of heroine that he will return to throughout his career – the witty woman. Most often seen in banter with her waiting-maid or a friend, this expansion of the female role was clearly very welcome to an audience perhaps tiring of the stereotype of talkative shrew (who must be tamed) or compliant near-silent young girl. In *Two Gentlemen* an early scene between the heroine and her maid is shown, immediately after the opening discussion of love and friendship between Proteus and Valentine accompanied by Speed's satirical comments on 'love'. In a dialogue that both complements and contrasts this scene, Julia shows that she too is subject to the irrational fits of romantic love, while Lucetta, her maid, performs the same debunking role as Speed, with realistic irony. Curiously, however, Shakespeare gives Julia two soliloquies in the course of this long scene, which allow the audience access to her inner life. Here we witness an emotional confusion, recognisable still today, about whether or not to accept a young man's advances:

> JULIA And yet I would I had o'erlooked the letter.
> It were a shame to call her back again
> And pray her to a fault for which I chid her.
> What fool is she, that knows I am a maid
> And would not force the letter to my view,
> Since maids, in modesty, say 'no' to that
> Which they would have the profferer construe 'ay'.
> . . . How angerly I taught my brow to frown
> When inward joy enforced my heart to smile.
> My penance is to call Lucetta back [etc.].
>
> (1.2.50–64)

There follows some amusing business in which Lucetta 'drops' the letter, they tussle over it, Julia melodramatically rips it up and then is reduced to trying to piece it together to read its contents.

The plot-structure of medieval romance, on which this play is based, ultimately allows very little freedom even to such an adventurous and passionate girl as Julia, who (like the heroines of many popular stories) gets into male disguise to follow her lover. There is some more banter between Julia and Lucetta as this ruse is planned, though the tone is overall more emotional (2.7). After this, Julia's comments to the Host and asides to the audience in the scene in which she sees her erstwhile lover serenading Silvia (4.2) have a pathos that foreshadows Viola in *Twelfth Night*. We hear her confide to the audience in not one but two soliloquies in 4.4, since she has no one else to ask for sympathy: their gist is, once again, the emotional confusion that arises out of being a young woman in a male culture.

> How many women would do such a message?
> Alas, poor Proteus, thou hast entertained
> A fox to be the shepherd of thy lambs.
> Alas, poor fool, why do I pity him
> That with his very heart despiseth me?
> Because he loves her, he despiseth me;
> Because I love him, I must pity him.
>
> (4.4.81–7)

Silvia, the play's other female protagonist, like many a fairy-tale heroine is locked into a tower at night by her father, though – as Juliet is to do in a play written a few years later – she makes her escape by behaving as a good daughter and going to confession. Both girls are powerless and virtually silent at the play's dénouement, as Valentine offers Silvia to his friend (who has just attempted to rape her), and Proteus, confronted with Julia (his 'page', Sebastian), switches again, declaring glibly, 'What is in Silvia's face but I may spy / More fresh in Julia's, with a constant eye?' (5.4.111–12). The stage is crowded with men at the play's end, organising the world in the way that suits them. The model of male behaviour underlying Petrarchan posturing is exposed for modern eyes, though its early audiences may simply have accepted it as an old-fashioned romance story. Today, setting it in any period in which society is under the control of a combination of smugly supreme males – rulers, fathers, and lovers – can make excellent sense. The play works particularly well in a 1950s setting – the last moment before the 'sexual revolution' began to disrupt the old gender ideologies.

A Midsummer Night's Dream

The same range of male figures is evident in the human world of *A Midsummer Night's Dream*. The young men of this play, Demetrius and Lysander, are as nearly indistinguishable as Valentine and Proteus. Shakespeare makes a joke of their emotional immaturity by objectifying the 'passion' of romantic love into a stage property, 'a little western flower', whose magic juice dropped into lovers' eyes makes them 'madly dote on the next live creature' that they see. Thus we have the absurd scenes, 2.2 and 3.2, in which, first, Lysander (the erstwhile lover of Hermia) awakens to make passionate declarations of love to Helena (who has hitherto hopelessly pursued Demetrius). He has the appropriate Petrarchan language on the tip of his tongue:

> LYSANDER Transparent Helena, nature shows art
> That through thy bosom makes me see thy heart.
> ... Reason becomes the marshal to my will[,]
> And leads me to your eyes, where I o'erlook
> Love's stories written in love's richest book.
>
> (2.2.110–11, 126–8)

Then, a few minutes later, Demetrius, supposedly also in love with Hermia, wakes to see Helena as his ideal beloved:

> DEMETRIUS O Helen, goddess, nymph, perfect, divine!
> To what, my love, shall I compare thine eyne?
> Crystal is muddy! O, how ripe in show
> Thy lips, those kissing cherries, tempting grow!
>
> (3.2.137–40)

But Helena has had enough of this deceiving rhetoric of courtly love, and speaks with articulate fury:

> O spite! O Hell! I see you all are bent
> To set against me for your merriment.
> If you were civil and knew courtesy,
> You would not do me thus much injury.
> Can you not hate me, as I know you do,
> But you must join in souls to mock me too?
> If you were men, as men you are in show,
> You would not use a gentle lady so,
> To vow, and swear, and superpraise my parts,
> When I am sure you hate me with your hearts.
>
> (3.2.145–54)

Not that this clear perception makes her own emotional life any easier: the next thing the audience witnesses is a girl-fight – an extended episode of physical comedy, scripted to include stage directions that direct the choreography of the scene. They play, particularly, on the comic potential of casting a tall girl and a short girl (or boys, originally) in the parts of Helena and Hermia:

> HELENA Fine, i'faith!
> Have you no modesty, no maiden shame,
> No touch of bashfulness? What, will you tear
> Impatient answers from my gentle tongue?
> Fie, fie, you counterfeit, you puppet, you!
> HERMIA 'Puppet'? Why so – Ay, that way goes the game.
> Now I perceive that she hath made compare
> Between our statures; she hath urged her height,
> And with her personage, her tall personage,
> Her height, forsooth, she hath prevailed with him.
> And are you grown so high in his esteem
> Because I am so dwarfish and so low?
> How low am I, thou painted maypole? Speak!
> How low am I? I am not yet so low
> But that my nails can reach unto thine eyes.
>
> (3.2.284–98)

It is important to note that neither of the girls has been anointed with the magic flower: their emotional lives are always more real, not scripted for them by literary conventions. When all four lovers awaken at the end of the midsummer's night (4.1), Demetrius remains in his enchanted state, so that he continues to see Helena as his true love (though he knows that something has cured him of a 'sickness', and that he has now 'come to [his] natural taste'). Lysander has had a second application of the love-juice, to return him to devotion to Hermia. The last words of the two girls occur in this scene – they don't speak during the play's grand finale – and both speeches have a certain ambiguity, a recognition that love is never easy, or its progress predictable:

> HERMIA Methinks I see these things with parted eye,
> When everything seems double.
> HELENA So methinks;
> And I have found Demetrius, like a jewel,
> Mine own, and not mine own.   (4.1.186–9)

In the play's fairy world, where the courtly romantic conventions are irrelevant, love is considerably more brutal. The love-juice dropped by Oberon on Titania's eyes carries a malevolent curse:

> OBERON What thou seest when thou dost wake,
> Do it for thy true-love take;
> Love and languish for his sake.
> Be it ounce or cat or bear,
> Pard, or boar with bristled hair
> In thy eye that shall appear
> When thou wak'st, it is thy dear.
> Wake when some vile thing is near!
>
> (2.2.33–40)

This will not be romantic love, but bestial lust. Oberon and Puck between them engineer Titania's waking to espy Bottom transformed with a donkey's head. The audience witnesses a coupling that contravenes inter-species taboos, class distinctions (working man and queen), and aesthetic taste ('My mistress with a monster is in love!' says Puck (3.2.6)). Nevertheless, their two scenes (3.1 and 4.1) have a charm that transcends the incongruous. They emphasise physical pleasure – music, food and drink, lovemaking:

> TITANIA Feed him with apricocks and dewberries,
> With purple grapes, green figs, and mulberries;
> The honey-bags steal from the humble-bees,
> And for night-tapers crop their waxen thighs,
> And light them at the fiery glow-worm's eyes,
> To have my love to bed and to arise.   (3.1.144–9)

It would be conceivable for a production to suggest that Titania, despite her reconciliation with the King of Fairies, regrets the loss of this interlude of pure physical pleasure. The last sight the audience has of her is very much that of a member of royalty doing her duty – blessing the 'bride-beds' of the lesser beings, the mortals. Often, particularly since the revolutionary production of the play by Peter Brook in 1969, Titania and Hippolyta are doubled, as are Oberon and Theseus. Both males rule their domains absolutely. Hippolyta has been 'wooed' with Theseus' sword ('and won thy love doing thee injuries', he announces complacently, 1.1.16–17); and arguably Oberon's triumph in the war for the little changeling boy (another disturbing aspect of the ego-driven world of the fairies) is won through *his* specialised weaponry, his knowledge of the magic flower and the advantages that he can gain through using it.

Working men: comic commentators

Just as in *Two Gentlemen of Verona*, the play's clowns provide a perspective from which romantic love can be satirised. Seductive though its ideology and aesthetics are, love is essentially impractical and ridiculous, as the climactic performance of 'Pyramus and Thisbe' demonstrates. What makes this critique even more pointed is the fact that it is presented in the form of a play: that is, the audience of *A Midsummer Night's Dream* registers, in all the hilarity of the preparations for and performance of 'Pyramus and Thisbe', that they are watching a sophisticated, complex, and satisfying piece of theatre. Theatre commenting upon itself is known as *metatheatricality*, and it is a trick that Shakespeare will return to in later plays (e.g. Hamlet's 'Mousetrap'). Only here and in *Love's Labour's Lost* does he allow largely uneducated working men to take centre-stage and by their earnest performance show us the charm, delights, and dangers of theatre: the way it tells us truths about ourselves and the ways we behave by *staging* behavioural habits and conventions; ultimately, by staging the discourses (the values and categories) by which we make sense of our society. The critique of the ruling classes (particularly of such men as Theseus and Egeus, authority figures who believe they have the right to run people's lives) is doubly pointed, coming from this unexpected quarter.

Yet, within the conventions of Elizabethan theatre, Shakespeare is simply expanding the role of the clown, the jester who can get away with satire on his masters and betters. In the cast of *A Midsummer Night's Dream* there are six 'Hard-handed men that work in Athens here' (5.1.72). This is a whole raft of clowns, with a storyline of their own – it is as important as the story of the runaway lovers or the quarrel of the fairies. Significantly, we meet the 'mechanicals', the working-class men, early in the play, in 1.2. The sense that in rehearsing a 'tragedy' they are commenting on the affected habits of the nobility is difficult to avoid, especially following the over-the-top performances by both Hermia and Helena of the lovestruck maiden (Helena's soliloquy at the end of 1.1 is a great opportunity for comic self-revelation). When we hear that the Athens workmen are to perform 'The most lamentable comedy and most cruel death of Pyramus and Thisbe', it is clear that the audience has permission to laugh at the behaviour of the noble lovers – 'lamentable' and 'cruel' are words that might feature in the self-indulgent complaints of all four lovers.

Each of the actors in Peter Quince's play has a strong concept of what it means to act a part in the theatre. Bottom is convinced that the leading man can play every role better than anyone else, and should be given the opportunity to do so – the hero, of course; his ladylove (if he can hide his face and play in 'a monstrous little voice'); *and* the lion, that epitome of masculine 'roaring'. Bottom, like many leading men, is obsessed with his costume – 'What beard were I best to play it in?' Flute the bellows-mender does *not* want to play Thisbe – 'Let not me play a woman. I have a beard coming.' How often must the adult members of the Chamberlain's Men have heard that complaint from the growing boy-apprentices! Snug the joiner is 'slow of study' – there's always one in every company, who has fallen into theatre by accident, and seems not to know what he's doing. There are multiple theatrical in-jokes here, which create a sophisticated dynamic of affectionate recognition between actors and audience; it is a far more complex relationship than that which we have with the 'picture-frame' *locus* in which the cartoonish story of the lovers is played out.

When the actors meet for their rehearsal in 3.1 their discussion immediately focuses on the basic philosophic problem presented by theatre: what is its relation to real life? Does it try and convince us that what we see on stage is 'really' happening, or should it always acknowledge its artificiality? These performers are so in awe of theatre's mimetic power that they opt for the safety of a framing prologue (or even two):

> BOTTOM I have a device to make all well. Write me a prologue, and let
> the prologue seem to say we will do no harm with our swords, and
> that Pyramus is not killed indeed; and for the more better assurance,
> tell them that I, Pyramus, am not Pyramus, but Bottom the weaver:
> this will put them out of fear.   (3.1.13–17)

Then there is the problem of how to produce realistic settings and lighting: either they can attempt to 'bring in a wall' and real moonlight – or, 'Some man or other must present' them symbolically. The decision that they opt for, to have actors perform these roles, is not only more sophisticated, it is also productive of some of the funniest moments in a very funny play. In the final performance (5.1) Snout's turn as Wall is an artistic triumph for him:

> Thus have I, Wall, my part dischargèd so;
> And being done, thus Wall away doth go.

But Starveling's attempt to match it as Moonshine sees his 'prologue' constantly interrupted by an audience that is more interested in showing off to each other. The impassioned actors of Pyramus and Thisbe (Bottom and Flute), and of course Snug's Lion, are unaffected by the antics of this ill-mannered audience. Their whole-hearted performance of the cliché-ridden 'lamentable tragedy' is far funnier than the smart witticisms of the young men in the audience – and, oddly, more moving, because we care about these actors who have worked so hard to make art. Peter Quince's prologue, repunctuated to make the sense that he so keenly desires to make, is a noble statement of the enduring work of the theatre:

> To show our simple skill,
> That is the true beginning of our end.
> . . . Our true intent is all for your delight.
> We are not here that you should here repent you.
> The actors are at hand; and, by their show
> You shall know all that you are like to know.
>   (5.1.110–17, repunctuated)

All this discussion of what we can call the 'theory of theatre' takes place between a group of clowns, not intellectuals; this fact foregrounds the artistic authority that actors have in the 'alternative' world of theatre. If the Chamberlain's Men normally employed only one professional clown, both here and in other early plays such as *Love's Labour's Lost* Shakespeare writes roles for at least another five actors that enabled them to display their comic skills and at the same time build bridges of knowing complicity between the stage and the audience: we share a sophisticated view of society, mediated by art, that the conventional noble or romantic characters are unable to imagine. Or are they? One of the play's most quoted speeches is that of Theseus in the last act, just as 'Pyramus and Thisbe' is about to be performed:

> I never may believe
> These antique fables, nor these fairy toys.
> Lovers and madmen have such seething brains,
> Such shaping fantasies, that apprehend
> More than cool reason ever comprehends.
> The lunatic, the lover, and the poet
> Are of imagination all compact:
> . . . The poet's eye, in a fine frenzy rolling,
> Doth glance from heaven to earth, from earth to heaven;
> And as imagination bodies forth
> The forms of things unknown, the poet's pen
> Turns them to shapes, and gives to airy nothing
> A local habitation and a name.   (5.1.2–17)

It is as though Shakespeare needed to have his most authoritative stage character (the Duke) give his stamp of approval to the process of artistic exploration of anarchic dreams and social reality that the past two or three hours have offered. As Hippolyta comments, from a more empathetic perspective:

> But all the story of the night told over,
> And all their minds transfigured so together,
> More witnesseth than fancy's images,
> And grows to something of great constancy;
> But, howsoever, strange and admirable.
>
> (5.1.23–7)

'Transfigured', 'strange and admirable': in this early play, Shakespeare anticipates the great speeches about the power of art that will issue from the mouth of the artist-magician, Prospero in *The Tempest*.

At about the same time that he wrote *A Midsummer Night's Dream* Shakespeare also wrote *The Most Excellent and Lamentable Tragedy of Romeo and Juliet*, based on Arthur Brooke's long poem of 1562 that he had already partly drawn on in *Two Gentlemen of Verona*. It is not possible to say whether the tragedy or comedy came first: what is indubitable is that 'Pyramus and Thisbe' affectionately lampoons the romantic tragedy, especially its touching double suicide conclusion. Most strikingly, *Romeo and Juliet*'s first half, until the death of the witty cynic Mercutio, is a comedy. Romeo's romantic tendencies are satirised (particularly by Mercutio); Peter the Clown and the Nurse provide classic vulgar comedy moments; and even the burgeoning love of Romeo and Juliet is treated with gentle irony as they work their way from Petrarchan clichés to something real and dangerous. Mercutio dies with a quip on his lips – 'Ask for me tomorrow, and you shall find me a grave man' (3.1.89–90) – and from that moment onwards, the play 'gallop[s] apace' (3.2.1) towards its tragic finale. It is as extraordinary an experiment in theatrical technique as the *Dream* is in metatheatre.

The Merchant of Venice

A Midsummer Night's Dream and *Romeo and Juliet* deal with the complications brought about by behaving according to the conventions of courtly love; *The Merchant of Venice*, written a year or so later, adds a very dark strain to the mix. 'What *is* love?' as Feste will sing in *Twelfth Night*. Bassanio courts his lady Portia according to the formula (she is beautiful, distant – and rich; he is charming, intelligent – and hungry), but he himself is involved in an earlier relationship – the love which the older man Antonio feels for him. Directors of individual productions can decide how much this love is returned, and whether it has a physical element (often, these days, it does), but there is no doubt that this is the emotional basis of the play (it is called The **Merchant** of *Venice*, i.e. Antonio). It comes to its climax in the courtroom confrontation between Shylock, Antonio, and Portia in Act 4, with Bassanio a helpless looker-on.

The play begins with Antonio: he is 'sad', and neither he nor his friends can articulate why this is so – to the assertion 'Why then, you are in love', he simply answers 'Fie, fie!' Yet when Bassanio arrives, and they are alone on stage, it is clear that Antonio has been waiting to hear of Bassanio's plans to woo Portia for her hand in marriage. It is not difficult to read a love-triangle here: Antonio is a rich older man, besotted with Bassanio, to whom he has already given much; Bassanio has now decided that he can do even better by marrying an heiress. The language in which this lover describes his lady – classical metaphors of fortune-hunting heroes mixed with the terms of modern commerce – indicates exactly how hard-headed Bassanio is in planning his marriage:

> In Belmont is a lady richly left,
> And she is fair and, – fairer than that word –
> Of wondrous virtues. Sometimes from her eyes
> I did receive fair speechless messages.
> Her name is Portia, nothing undervalued
> To Cato's daughter, Brutus' Portia.
> Nor is the wide world ignorant of her worth;
> For the four winds blow in from every coast
> Renownèd suitors, and her sunny locks
> Hang on her temples like a golden fleece,
> Which makes her seat of Belmont Colchos' strand,
> And many Jasons come in quest of her.
> O my Antonio, had I but the means
> To hold a rival place with one of them,
> I have a mind presages me such thrift
> That I should questionless be fortunate.
>
> (1.1.160–75)

'Richly', 'worth', 'golden', 'thrift', 'fortune' – and she fancies him. Similarly, in a previous speech Bassanio has spoken of his boyish games in terms designed to persuade Antonio to 'hazard' a margin loan for Bassanio's speculative invest- ment in courtship (1.1.139–51). Antonio acknowledges what they both know: that he would not refuse Bassanio anything; and, not having the money to hand, offers to be guarantor for a loan. And so the play's other dark strand is intimated by the end of its first scene. The loan will come from the embittered, ghettoised Shylock.

We don't, however, meet Shylock just yet; Shakespeare first takes the oppor- tunity to show the 'real' Portia, not the metaphorical golden princess. In 1.2 we have a scene such as he had already written successfully for mistress and maid in *Two Gentlemen* (at exactly the same point, 1.2). Interestingly, Portia also claims to be 'aweary of this great world' – which we might gloss as unhappy with the world structured as it is, in which 'the will of a living daughter [is] curbed by the will of a dead father'. She is, we learn, literally a lottery prize: her portrait is hidden in one of the three caskets of gold, silver, and lead; and her father has decreed that she *will* love the suitor who chooses correctly. Shakespeare's use of this ancient folk-motif offers as powerful a critique of the mythology of romantic love as that displayed in the commercial metaphors of Bassanio's speech quoted above. These two have their work cut out for them to convince the audience that they will make an emotionally satisfying love-match.

One way of doing this – of making the audience like and care about Portia – is to show that she is witty, intelligent, and full of vitality; which is exactly what we see in the remainder of the scene as she and Nerissa between them mercilessly analyse the failings of the current crop of suitors – sports-mad callow youths, drunks, self-important pseudo-intellectuals, narcissists, and dimwits (categories which would easily fit with a modern-dress production). We have a couple of fine examples of the latter types in the two suitors, Morocco and Aragon, who respectively choose the gold and silver caskets in scenes in Act 2. No wonder that Portia is momentarily lost for words when Nerissa mentions the 'soldier and scholar' Bassanio, who seems to be 'the best deserving a fair lady'. Although the audience may know more of his weaknesses than she does, Bassanio at least stands out well in the array of suitors; and Portia desires him.

This is made clear in their first scene together (3.2), the scene in which Bassanio eventually chooses the (correct) lead casket, possibly helped by the song which Portia has commanded, with its insistent rhymes on 'lead'. Portia's blank verse here, opening the scene, is hesistant and repetitive, expressive of much less self-confidence than the prose or verse of her earlier scenes:

> I pray you tarry, pause a day or two
> Before you hazard, for in choosing wrong,
> I lose your company; therefore forbear a while.
> There's something tells me, but it is not love,
> I would not lose you; . . .
> One half of me is yours, the other half yours –
> Mine own, I would say: but if mine then yours,
> And so all yours . . .
> I speak too long, but 'tis to peize [retard] the time,
> To eche [eke] it, and to draw it out in length,
> To stay you from election.   (3.2.1–24)

Both lovers have a number of strikingly long speeches in this scene; for actors, they are a gift that enables them to show the almost hysterical nature of their characters' desire, their need to get this right, to be together. Shakespeare used the same technique in the 'balcony scene' of *Romeo and Juliet*, where there is a gentle joke about the young lovers who cannot bear to be out of each other's company, so that they keep coming back to say goodnight. Thus, although both Portia and Juliet in these scenes embody the remote love-object of Petrarchan poetry (the 'pedestal' symbolised by casket or balcony), their *speech* shows them to be figures of flesh and blood, who are extremely keen to eliminate the physical distance between themselves and their lovers. Bassanio, too, is transformed by desire, unable at this point to call up a proper classical metaphor:

> Madam, you have bereft me of all words.
> Only my blood speaks to you in my veins,
> And there is such confusion in my powers,
> As after some oration fairly spoke
> By a belovèd prince there doth appear
> Among the buzzing, pleasèd multitude,
> Where every something being blent together,
> Turns to a wild of nothing, save of joy
> Expressed, and not expressed.   (3.2.175–83)

The scene moves briefly back to broad comedy: Graziano and Nerissa announce their engagement. But then Salerio arrives with the message that Antonio has lost his money and is threatened with the enactment of Shylock's vengeful bond. The emotional triangle foreshadowed in the play's first scene now has life-or-death consequences.

Bassanio, the nominal hero, cannot solve the problem. Portia can – she has money. More, she has wit, intelligence, and determination. Her decision to go to the court disguised as a young male lawyer is a major paradigm shift from the earlier breeches-role of Julia in *Two Gentlemen*. Whereas Julia was following the model of the medieval and Renaissance stories, in which young women routinely disguised themselves as pages in order to follow their faithless lovers, Portia makes the decision in order to intervene in a situation of real-world danger. Her disguise is that of a professional man who has a right to take part in the business of the 'great world'. Her energy has found a proper outlet: no longer on a pedestal, she can wield the power that she knows she has, even if society as a whole would disapprove.

Shylock

Shylock can be played as simply the comic villain in this romance; and the scant evidence up to the mid-eighteenth century suggests that this was often the case (it was not, however, a popular play for revival after the theatres reopened at the Restoration in 1660). Played as a caricature Jew, with hooked nose and claw-like hands, he had much in common with the figures of ultimately impotent evil that appear in the medieval Christian Mystery plays. His immediate predecessor on the English stage was Christopher Marlowe's Jew of Malta, significantly named Barabas (the criminal who was released instead of Jesus). Barabas is a monstrous and murderous villain, with an occasional line in black wit; he gets his rightful (and comic) comeuppance by being drowned in a cauldron. At no point is the audience asked to take him seriously as a human being. Shakespeare was familiar with this hit play of Marlowe's, but his decision to write his own 'Jew-play' and graft it onto the form of romantic comedy produced a hybrid that took both genres in unprecedented directions.

Shylock in fact has very few lines that align him simply with the caricature that appears in medieval Catholic superstition. His first scene, 1.3, might be thought of as offering the Elizabethan audience the Jew they were familiar with from Marlowe's and other plays, at least to start with – lines such as this aside to the audience about Antonio:

> How like a fawning publican he looks!
> I hate him for he is a Christian;
> . . . If I can catch him once upon the hip,
> I will feed fat the ancient grudge I bear him.
> He hates our sacred nation, and he rails
> Even there where merchants most do congregate
> On me, my bargains, and my well-won thrift
> Which he calls interest. Cursed be my tribe
> If I forgive him!   (1.3.33–44)

Soon, however, in this long scene, Shylock is revealing a more complex personality. He offers the Christians an ad-hoc lecture on the Jewish virtue of 'thrift', i.e. thoughtful planning in order to increase one's wealth – something that we know already is quite foreign to Bassanio's lordly assumption that if he shoots a few arrows in the same direction, somehow some good fortune will come of it (the dartboard approach to personal wealth creation). He then launches into a speech that has such passion behind it that the audience can infer he has been waiting a long time for the opportunity to utter it:

> Signor Antonio, many a time and oft
> In the Rialto you have rated me
> About my monies and my usances . . .

It's a speech about being the victim of racial abuse, and it returns, obsessively, to the graphic image of the Christian spitting on the Jew:

> What should I say to you? Should I not say
> 'Hath a dog money? Is it possible
> A cur can lend three thousand ducats?' Or
> Shall I bend low, and in a bondman's key,
> With bated breath and whisp'ring humbleness,
> Say this:
> 'Fair sir, you spat on me on Wednesday last,
> You spurned me such a day, another time
> You called me dog: and for these courtesies
> I'll lend you thus much monies.'
>
> (1.3.98–121)

Antonio is arrogantly unmoved by this. His response is that of the bully: 'I am as like to call thee so again, / To spit on thee again, to spurn thee too.' The audience is surely on the eloquent victim's side at this point. But notwithstanding the insults, Shylock offers to lend Antonio the money, and proposes 'in a merry sport' that he nominate as bond 'an equal pound of [his] fair flesh to be cut off and taken / In what part of your body so pleaseth me.' This 'merry bond', as he points out, will not profit him; it is offered as a gesture of 'friendship'. It is also offered, we might say, as a macabre reminder of the superstitions that medieval Christians held about Jews (sacrificial child-murder being the most persistent). It challenges the audience: do we take the threat seriously (Bassanio does: 'I like not fair terms and a villain's mind') or do we dismiss it as Antonio does? Whose side are we on?

The problem is – and this is where theatre has a particular advantage in presenting moral and ethical issues – that fragile human bodies are the frontline soldiers of grand ideologies. Whether it is Portia suffering the indignity of being a prize in a lottery, Shylock being abused and spat on, or Antonio at the point of a crazed and enraged Shylock's knife, the powerful members of society maintain their control by sacrificing the powerless and calling it 'the law'. At exactly the centre of the play (3.1), Shylock has a memorable and often-quoted speech, which encapsulates this perception: he is both a generic human body *and* a member of an ideological group.

I am a Jew. Hath not a Jew eyes? Hath not a Jew hands, organs,
dimensions, senses, affections, passions? Fed with the same food, hurt
with the same weapons, subject to the same diseases, healed by the same
means, warmed and cooled by the same winter and summer as a
Christian is? If you prick us, do we not bleed? If you tickle us, do we not
laugh? If you poison us, do we not die? And if you wrong us, shall we not
revenge? If we are like you in the rest, we will resemble you in that. If a
Jew wrong a Christian, what is his humility? Revenge. If a Christian
wrong a Jew, what should his sufferance be by Christian example? Why,
revenge! The villainy you teach me I will execute, and it shall go hard but
I will better the instruction.   (3.1.46–57)

Wars, therefore, will continue, as ideology negates shared humanity. This is
why the confrontation between Shylock and Portia over Antonio's body is so
powerful. It is an ideological confrontation – Christian New Testament 'mercy'
versus Jewish Old Testament 'revenge' – but it is played out in the bodies and
words of two powerless figures in the overarching social structure, patriarchal
Venice: a woman, and a Jew from the ghetto. One of the most interesting small
points of the dramaturgy of this scene is that the titular authority, the Duke (or
Doge) of Venice, hands over his authority to the young lawyer, not knowing
that she is a woman. But the audience knows.

Neither Portia nor Shylock is a completely sympathetic figure in this confrontation (4.1). Portia's beautiful speech on the quality of mercy (the other
most-quoted speech in the play) continues to address Shylock offensively as
'Jew' rather than as an individual; and Shylock, similarly, reverts to his caricature role as monster, ostentatiously sharpening his knife on the sole of his shoe.
If this is comedy, it is black and discomfiting about the way ideology perverts
our behaviour. By the end of the confrontation Shylock's punishment, that 'he
presently become a Christian' cannot be read in any way as comic, since it calls
into play an ideology that no member of the play's original audience would
dare to question (by contrast, Barabas' death in a cauldron – his own plot gone
wrong – is macabrely funny).

It is virtually impossible in the post-Holocaust world to see Shylock as anything other than tragic. Driven to revenge against a 'Christian' community
that despises him, that destroys his family and his business, Shylock cracks
and offers symbolic violence when the opportunity arises.[2] In fact as early as
the mid-nineteenth century, this view of Shylock often prevailed: productions
of the play would end with the court scene and the destruction of the tragic
outsider. Act 5's return to romantic comedy was simply not played.

Nevertheless the play as written and printed (there was a Quarto published
in Shakespeare's lifetime, so it must have been popular) does have an Act 5, and

does resolve the complications of the romantic plot, complications which have been signalled at the end of Act 4 with Bassanio and Graziano giving away the rings their fiancées had given them. What is brought back into play here is the issue with which the play began: the conflict between the bonds of homosocial male society[3] and those of heterosexual marriage, a theme that preoccupied Shakespeare throughout much of his career.

Act 5 begins curiously: it looks like a romantic moonlight scene between Lorenzo and Jessica (though we might remember that Jessica is Shylock's daughter 'stolen' from him by the Christian youths) – but their lyrical dialogue, 'In such a night . . .' is all about faithless lovers from ancient mythology. Romantic love is fragile when it is framed by opposing ideologies, as all these examples are (Romeo and Juliet could easily be added). The dialogue finally turns away from the disharmony of human societies to the harmony of the spheres, and, more particularly, to its representation in the earthly form of music, which is then played. As Lorenzo says,

> naught so stockish, hard, and full of rage,
> But music for the time doth change his nature.
> The man that hath no music in himself,
> Nor is not moved with concord of sweet sounds,
> Is fit for treasons, stratagems, and spoils;
> The motions of his spirit are dull as night,
> And his affections dark as Erebus.
> Let no such man be trusted.   (5.1.81–8)

Music here stands for the work of the artist in general: Lorenzo refers to the work of 'the poet' who first told the story of Orpheus. This moment is strikingly like the moment in Act 5 of *A Midsummer Night's Dream* when Theseus and Hippolyta discuss the imagination. In both cases there is a sense of the playwright summing up, drawing attention subtly to the pleasurable, thought-provoking but ultimately safe experience that the actors have given us over the preceding two or three hours. Portia's entry lines chime beautifully with this mood:

> That light we see is burning in my hall.
> How far that little candle throws his beams!
> So shines a good deed in a naughty world.
>   (5.1.89–91)

The play then mutates quickly into farce, a movement that foregrounds the 'merry war' of the sexes and reminds us that for all the claims of, on the one hand, ideology, and on the other, money, it is heterosexual desire that actually makes the world go round. Bawdy jokes about who has control of the 'rings' raise the energy of the play as it comes to its end, obscuring, perhaps, the memory of the dark events of Act 4. But, for those who look more carefully, there is just one person on stage at the end of the play without a lover – Antonio. In a poignant but neat irony, the triumphant Portia insists that Antonio should be the intermediary in the final return of her ring to Bassanio: heterosexuality, 'romance' – however qualified by financial motives – has triumphed.[4]

Chapter 4

Comedy and language

Love's Labour's Lost

The 'great feast of languages'

Plays are made of words and actions; in terms of actions, comedies, as we have seen, focus on behaviour – farcical or social – that has the potential for comic effects. What of the words that the characters speak? Late Elizabethan England was fascinated by language and its potential for persuasion, poetry, argument, and entertainment. As Shakespeare settled into his career as a playwright he took the opportunity to write a comedy that reflects almost obsessively upon the very material of his art – words and their power. Why a comedy? Language is the essence of social communication; through language we create a public identity, and attempt, using this most subtle and variable of instruments, to attain our desires. If courtship is our business, our linguistic competency is vital: '*Listen* to me, *look* at me, *love* me!' it says. And the potential for getting it laughably wrong is immense. So, in this chapter, we will follow Shakespeare's reflections, in an almost plot-free play, on the role of language in the human community – a community that is dependent on courtship for its continuity.

In 1598 there appeared a quarto volume with this title-page: 'A Pleasant Conceited Comedie called, Loues labors lost. As it was presented before her highnes this last Christmas. Newly corrected and augmented By W. Shakespere.' This was the first play-text to have Shakespeare's name on the title-page; it is one of several contemporary signs of his fame as a wordsmith, and it also indicates that this particular play had already had a successful public career, and had been performed before the Queen. Scholars believe, on stylistic and topical evidence, that it was probably written 1593–5, a little before *A Midsummer Night's Dream*. 'A pleasant *conceited* comedy' – that is, it proudly advertises the fact that it is full of word-play ('conceits', or witty concepts – they are etymologically the same).[1] It reflects the excitement about the English language, and language in general, that came to a head in a number of theoretical treatises published in

the last quarter of the century. At the same time the first English dictionaries –
advertised as lists of 'hard words' with their explanations – were published.
John Florio's *A Worlde of Wordes* dates from 1598, and it was so successful that
he published *Queen Anna's New World of Words* in 1611. All literate people quite
suddenly had access to a plethora of handbooks and discourses and exemplars
on rhetoric. Henry Peacham's *The Garden of Eloquence*, for example, was first
published in 1577, and issued in a revised edition in 1593. Highly literate
gentlemen, like the lords in *Love's Labour's Lost*, were trying their hands at
sonnet-sequences (Shakespeare's own sonnets were circulated in manuscript
in the 1590s before being published in 1609). Novels and romances that gloried
in their linguistic copiousness were fashionable successes: Lyly's *Euphues* (1578–
80) gave its name to a type of florid writing, euphuism, imitated in Thomas
Lodge's *Rosalynd* (1590), which Shakespeare used as his source text for *As You
Like It*.

London's population was rising fast – to double by 1620 (to 400,000, despite
the high death rate associated with a crowded and unsanitary city). Many
dialects and foreign words brought in by merchants and travellers were entering the mix of the capital's speech. Shakespeare's own vocabulary has been
calculated at more than 25,000 words – two or three times the ordinary adult's
vocabulary. He uses latinisms, French words, English slang, vernacular, and
dialect, as well as inventing compounds and freely transforming nouns into
verbs and verbs into nouns. Arguably this audacious way with words con-
tributed to his rising popularity, along with the dramaturgic brilliance and
acute social and psychological observation that enabled him to make 'pleasant
conceited' comedies and exciting history plays out of the fashion for eloquence.[2]
The unprecedented fluidity and richness of the English language is commented
on specifically in *Love's Labour's Lost*, at the beginning of Act 5 scene 1 (i.e. near
the play's end, when the audience has been delighted – or assaulted – with
'conceits' for two hours), when Holofernes and Nathaniel converse tipsily in
shreds of Latin, their topic spelling and pronunciation. The clever page Moth
comments, 'They have been at a great feast of languages and stolen the scraps.'

Holofernes the pedant wants Latin to dictate the rules of English spelling.
Given the contemporary fluidity of spelling and punctuation, punning is positively addictive in this period. Homonyms (the same word and spelling for
different things, e.g. *march*, meaning a military walk, a month, a frontier)
are not distinct from homophones (words with the same sound but different
spelling, e.g. *die* and *dye*): only the context supplies meaning. The settling of
modern spelling was largely an eighteenth-century project, a rationalist attempt
to eliminate ambiguity in the language. Shakespeare and his audience seemingly preferred the fertile *dis*order of 'orthography' (spelling), in which double

and triple meanings emerged almost by chance, demonstrating the glorious copiousness of language, its 'great feast'.[3]

Rules of rhetoric

One of the most interesting and influential of the treatises on language was a book called *The Arte of English Poesie*, published in 1589. The author (probably George Puttenham) writes at length about *appropriate* language, arguing the case for southern English as the standard of speech and writing – that which is spoken by 'civil' people in London (and 'the shires lying about London within lx. [60] miles'). He is equally fascinated by and wary of change: 'strange terms of other languages . . . [and] dark words . . . not usual nor well sounding, though they be daily spoken in Court'. He justifies his own use in the treatise of several new words, because the old ones just don't have the right nuance: 'I cannot see how we may spare them, whatsoever fault we find with ink-horn terms, for our speech wanteth [lacks] words to such sense so well to be used.'[4]

Book III of Puttenham's work is concerned with 'Ornament'. Poets, or 'makers', he argues, should fashion their language and style,

> to such purpose as it may delight and allure as well the mind as the ear of the hearers with a certain novelty and strange manner of conveyance, disguising it no little from the ordinary and accustomed; nevertheless making it nothing the more unseemly or misbecoming, but rather decenter and more agreeable to any civil ear and understanding.

Similarly, public speeches 'ought to be figurative; and, if they be not, do greatly disgrace the cause and purpose of the speaker and writer'. There is an expectation, that is, that any educated character speaking on the stage will utilise the tropes and figures of rhetoric; Puttenham argues that *lustre* and *energy* are provided by effective ornamentation. Ultimately, syntax, or the meaningful arrangement of words in sentences, relied more on vigour than on perfect grammar, and the art of rhetoric provided a system that created meaning primarily through acoustic patterning: the brilliant and energetic deployment of figures of speech.[5]

Rhetoric was taught in grammar schools and universities, with Latin as the exemplary language. Only boys went to 'grammar' (=Latin) school and university; only boys formally learnt rhetoric. Only the male characters in *Love's Labour's Lost* are in love with the sound of their own voices uttering the productions of their over-educated brains, though their female opponents are just as clever, and demonstrably even wittier – using their wit often to deflate the pomposity of the men's hot-house culture.

Love's Labour's Lost is a play about characters who are fascinated by rhetoric, and delighted with the copiousness of late sixteenth-century language. To be educated in rhetoric and use it well is to have access to cultural power. But – as always when power is in question – there is the danger of mistaking the instrument for the source of power itself. The play demonstrates that a sense of moral and spiritual decorum or fitness is ultimately more powerful – and admirable. Always, says Puttenham, it is necessary in speech to have 'a special regard to all circumstances of the person, place, time, cause, and purpose'. In *Love's Labour's Lost* each character shows his or her social and emotional fitness by their relation to language. That they do this in the course of a traditional comedy plot and structure is a sign of Shakespeare's early mastery of dramatic form.

The clowns

In *Love's Labour's Lost*, for the first time in Shakespeare's work (and just before *A Midsummer Night's Dream*), there is a 'copia' of clowns, of many different types, all able to make the audience laugh with their satire of their betters – sometimes wittily, sometimes unwittingly. Each has a degree of education and/or status, which differentiates and points the satire.

Don Armado, 'a refined traveller of Spain' (we meet this type again in *The Merchant of Venice*, in the Prince of Aragon), combines the commedia figure of the braggart soldier with a quality peculiar to this play: his comical affectations take the form of total subservience to the examples of rhetoric handbooks. He is, as the King says,

> A man in all the world's new fashion planted,
> That hath a mint of phrases in his brain,
> One who the music of his own vain tongue
> Doth ravish like enchanting harmony.
>
> (1.1.163–7)[6]

His character is well represented by the letter he sends the King accusing Costard of consorting with the 'wench' Jaquenetta. A brief sample gives the flavour:

> So it is, besieged with sable-coloured melancholy, I did commend the black-oppressing humour to the most wholesome physic of thy healthgiving air; and, as I am a gentleman, betook myself to walk. The time when? About the sixth hour, when beasts most graze, birds best peck, and men sit down to that nourishment which is called supper. So much for the time when. Now for the ground which – which, I mean, I walked upon. It is yclept thy park.   (1.1.227–35)

The fantastical flourishes of rhetorical figures serve Armado as a substitute for the sword-flourishes of the braggart soldier. In love with Jaquenetta himself, he concludes that his campaign will have to be literary:

> Adieu, valour; rust, rapier; be still, drum; for your manager is in love;
> yea, he loveth. Assist me, some extemporal god of rhyme, for I am sure I
> shall turn sonnet. Devise, wit; write, pen; for I am for whole volumes in
> folio.   (1.2.172–6)

This, of course, is exactly the decision taken not much later by the King and his three lords when they realise that they too are in love, despite their first-act vow not to see women for three years. Those young men are, like Don Armado, blind to the ridiculousness of their behaviour.

Three village worthies each have a modicum of education. Holofernes, the schoolmaster, thinks that Latin phrases give him status (and of course they do, in the village). Nathaniel the curate plays Holofernes' enthusiastic echo, producing, for example, some amusing double-entendres as he tries to keep up with the schoolmaster in 4.2. Dull, the village constable who is the third character in this scene, has an elementary professional grasp of legal discourse – he knows what he *should* sound like – but like Shakespeare's later creation constable Dogberry (in *Much Ado*), he often gets the words slightly wrong, creating unconscious puns as he does so, as in his inability to distinguish between 'allusion', 'collusion', and 'pollution' in 4.2.38–44.

Costard, a rustic clown, may be 'unlettered' (illiterate) but he can play with words with some panache. That is, he has oral competence, as befits a professional clown or jester, who has the freedom to exchange banter even with the King. In this fast-moving dialogue with its boom-tish conclusion the King is cast as the straight man:

> KING Did you hear the proclamation?
> COSTARD I do confess much of the hearing it, but little of the marking
> of it.
> KING It was proclaimed a year's imprisonment to be taken with a
> wench.
> COSTARD I was taken with none, sir, I was taken with a damsel.
> KING Well, it was proclaimed damsel.
> COSTARD This was no damsel neither, sir; she was a virgin.
> KING It is so varied too, for it was proclaimed virgin.
> COSTARD If it were, I deny her virginity. I was taken with a maid.
> KING This maid will not serve your turn, sir.
> COSTARD This maid will serve my turn, sir.   (1.1.272–86)

Nathan Lane's performance of this clown role (as a travelling showman), in Kenneth Branagh's 2000 film of the play, is an excellent example of the durability of clowning, and of its ability to bypass class hierarchies. Moth, the boy attending Don Armado, is practising to be a just such a jester at court (Armado calls him 'well-educated infant', 1.2.90). Don Armado is delighted with Moth's 'sweet smoke of rhetoric', positively encouraging it despite Moth's cheekiness about Armado's love-life:

> MOTH Negligent student! Learn her by heart.
> ARMADO By heart and in heart, boy.
> MOTH And out of heart, master; all those three I will prove.
> ARMADO What wilt thou prove?
> MOTH A man, if I live; and this, 'by', 'in', and 'without', upon the instant. 'By' heart you love her, because your heart cannot come by her. 'In' heart you love her because your heart is in love with her. And 'out' of heart you love her, being out of heart that you cannot enjoy her.   (3.1.32–42)

On the evidence of his facility with puns and rhetoric, and of his general ability to dart about, observing all, Moth might well grow up to take the professional name Touchstone or Feste.

Courtly language and gender

Castiglione, in *The Courtier*, is anxious to ensure that the wit of 'civility' is not confused with that of professional clowns: 'in the first kind of merry talk a man must in his protestation and counterfeiting take heed that he be not like common jesters and parasites, and such as with fond matters move men to laugh'. Of course a gentleman should be witty (and Castiglione spends considerable time discussing appropriate wit); but Castiglione is also interested in the position of women in relation to language. His discussants raise the problem of bawdy talk, and an unexpected realism emerges:

> M. Bernard [concluding an anecdote dependent on double-entendre] . . . You may see the taunt was witty, but because it was in presence of women it appeared bawdy and not to be spoken.
>   Then spake the Lord Gaspar Pallavicin: Women have none other delight but to hear of such matters, and yet will you deprive them of it. And for my part I have been ready to blush for shame at words which women have spoken to me oftener than men.
>
> (Castiglione, *The Courtier*, Book 2)

  The dialogue form in which this treatise is written includes several ladies. The Duchess, who (like the Princess in *Love's Labour's Lost*) is of the highest status, concludes this section of the discussion by challenging the theorising men to turn their minds to the definition of a 'Gentlewoman . . . equal with the Courtier in virtue', by which she means not only good behaviour but also intelligence and wit. Her ally, the Lady Emilia, has the Rosaline-like role of tarter comment: 'I pray God it fall not to our lot to give this enterprise to any confederate with the Lord Gaspar, least he fashion us for a gentlewoman of the Court, one that can do nought else but look to the kitchen and spin.' In a move that seems to anticipate Shakespeare's dramaturgy in *Love's Labour's Lost*, the ladies have the decisive last word in the day's discussion, sending the gentlemen away to prepare their wits for the next day's conversations: 'And when she had so said, they arose all upon their feet, and taking their leave reverently of the Duchess every man withdrew him to his lodging.'

Shakespeare's play stages this ongoing debate about language and gender, to be engaged with by an audience whose members themselves might not be particularly literate, but who were certainly fascinated by the contemporary debates on education, language, and decorum. The perspicacious young Moth summarises the standard view: 'My father's wit and my mother's tongue assist me!' (1.2.91) – that is, wit comes from education (available only to men), volubility ('tongue') is natural to women. The play tests, and ultimately demolishes, the usefulness of this gendered view of language and culture.

Act 1 shows us the men, both nobles and rustics. The King's speech, opening the play, exudes authority and confidence, dependent on familiar masculine concepts ('fame', 'honour', 'eternity', etc.):

> Let fame, that all hunt after in their lives,
> Live registered upon our brazen tombs,
> And then grace us in the disgrace of death;
> When, spite of cormorant devouring Time,
> Th'endeavour of this present breath may buy
> That honour which shall bate his scythe's keen edge,
> And make us heirs of all eternity.
> Therefore, brave conquerors – for so you are,
> That war against your own affections
> And the huge army of the world's desires –
> Our late edict shall strongly stand in force.
> Navarre shall be the wonder of the world;
> Our court shall be a little academe,
> Still and contemplative in living art.   (1.1.1–14)

The fact that this is basically an absurd proposition – that they should shut themselves off from the world (and women) for three years in order to 'study' – is disguised by the speech's consciously crafted rhetorical structure. The syntax – 'Let fame . . . Therefore . . . now subscribe' – allows for no objections; and the powerful tropes ('brazen tombs', 'cormorant devouring Time', 'scythe's keen edge', 'huge army of the world's desires') evoke a traditional masculine mind-set of battle and honour. It is all supported by seductive alliteration and a pounding rhythm that forges inexorably to the end of each line. It is a fine piece of public rhetoric, and it takes some time for Biron, the cleverest thinker of this group of courtiers, to come up with some qualifications to the absurd idea. This he does in a series of quasi-sonnets, which are even more complex rhetorical structures, delighting particularly in the figures of chiasmus and antithesis, and of course in rhyme:

> painfully to pore upon a book
> To seek the light of truth, while truth the while
> Doth falsely blind the eyesight of his look.
> Light seeking light doth light of light beguile;
> So, ere you find where light in darkness lies,
> Your light grows dark by losing of your eyes.
>
> (1.1.74–9)

As the King drily comments, 'How well he's read, to reason against reading.' Biron may be a non-conformist, but he likes to show off his linguistic brilliance, and he certainly doesn't want to be excluded from this elite male company.

The contrast with the opening of Act 2, the entry of the ladies, could hardly be stronger. Their blank verse, while not lacking elegance, is much more straightforward plain English; it foregrounds facts rather than theories or conventions. The Princess explicitly rejects Boyet's flowery language, with a sly dig at his linguistic vanity:

> Good Lord Boyet, my beauty, though but mean,
> Needs not the painted flourish of your praise.
> Beauty is bought by judgment of the eye,
> Not uttered by base sale of chapmen's tongues.
> I am less proud to hear you tell my worth
> Than you much willing to be counted wise
> In spending your wit in the praise of mine.
>
> (2.1.13–19)

The long conversation that then follows between the ladies and the lords (who come out to greet them, immediately breaking their vow of no conversation with women) is striking for its combination of good sense and flirtatious wit, on both sides. Unavoidably, courtship has begun. We are watching a dance-like interaction between the gentlemen and the ladies, in which, at various points, couples come to the front of the stage to chat and give the audience a taste of what attracts them to each other. (Shakespeare repeats this pattern in the masque scene, 2.1, of *Much Ado About Nothing*.)

Act 3 is a single scene giving the centre of the play to the three major clowns, Armado, Moth and Costard, whose linguistic characteristics I discussed above. It is, largely, delightful nonsense – many of the play's most memorable jokes occur here. Like the mid-point scenes of many of the comedies, it has very little to do with the plot and a great deal to do with theme: in this case, language and its uses and abuses. At the end of the scene Biron comes on, and the minor complication concerning the two love-letters (Armado's and Biron's) is set in train via the illiterate Costard, who is delighted to receive both a 'remuneration' and a 'gardon' [guerdon] for his pains (he translates these latinisms into what the words mean for him – three farthings and a shilling). The scene ends with Biron alone on stage, demonstrating his powerful rhetorical skills (and the habits of thinking they inculcate) in a soliloquy that is at once misogynistic and self-disgusted: 'And I, forsooth, in love! . . .' The sub-text of the soliloquy is that nature has defeated nurture: sexual desire has proved irresistible even to this proud intellectual.

In the next scene we see the ladies very much at home in nature. They are supposedly going hunting (normally, a masculine activity), but the scene is really an opportunity for them to show off their wit and talk about sex and love amongst themselves. Boyet, the only gentleman in the Princess's retinue, is clearly a somewhat effeminate figure and therefore safe ('Monsieur the Nice', Biron calls him: 'Nay, he can sing / A mean most meanly, and, in ushering, / Mend him who can. The ladies call him sweet' (5.2.325–9)). He provides cues for the ladies to indulge in extended bawdy talk and double-entendre. Castiglione would probably have enjoyed this scene; a period production might even costume Boyet as the author of *The Courtier*.

A further strong contrast is the following scene (4.3), one that shows all the lords admitting that they are victims of love. Things have changed a good deal since 1.1's presumptuous declarations of superhuman self-control. Beginning with the still self-disgusted soliloquising Biron, as each lord comes on stage it becomes clear that they remain conscious performers of literary attitudes. Each lord (beginning with the King himself) arrives, thinking himself alone, to indulge himself reading aloud the poem he is writing to his lady-love; then he has to quickly hide – and overhear the next lord's poetical efforts. The net result is farcical: four grown men trying to hide on a bare stage increasingly covered with abandoned sheets of paper. Biron, who thinks himself unassailable, pompously 'step[s] forth to whip hypocrisy', but is soon brought down even more humiliatingly by the entry of Jaquenetta and Costard with Biron's letter to Rosaline. The end-result of this scene of exposure is that the young men accept that love has conquered them all. The King asks Biron to use his rhetorical skills to 'prove / Our loving lawful and our faith not torn', which Biron does in a lengthy pseudo-legal blank-verse speech. His rhetoric reinforces their masculine self-image – 'Have at you then, affection's men-at-arms' – and they decide to be 'soldiers' *for* love, not against it. The ladies are to be wooed by 'revels, dances, masques, and merry hours', all performed by the men. This new variety of exhibitionism can produce highly comical results if, as is common in productions, the 'Russians', in heavy fake beards and boots, attempt a cossack dance.

The lords' efforts are treated as child's play by the ladies, who easily bamboozle them by masking and wearing each other's 'favours' (gifts from their lovers), while engaging in witty banter with the men. The serious question raised here is how well do these gentlemen know the ladies they claim to love uniquely; they have, in fact, a long way to go before they deserve acceptance by the more mature women. As the Princess remarks, 'We are wise girls to mock our lovers so' (5.2.58). This perception underlies the curious moment a little later when Rosaline declares (to the King, who thinks she is the Princess),

> Since you are strangers, and come here by chance,
> We'll not be nice. Take hands. We will not dance.
>
> (5.2.218–19)

Dancing is a sign, in the comedies yet to be written, of mutual harmony and suitability: we see characters who 'fit' each other. One of Jerome Kern's great songs in the Fred Astaire and Ginger Rogers film, *Roberta*, is 'I won't dance, don't ask me'. The audience of the film knows that Fred and Ginger will end up together, but Fred's character has to grow up considerably before the ecstatic dance that ends the film. Here, the King asks, uncomprehending, 'Why take we hands then?' and Rosaline replies with a civility and wisdom that he is yet incapable of, 'Only to part friends.'[7]

When the ladies reveal that they were not fooled by the 'Russians', and that moreover they themselves were disguised, Biron, speaking for all the men, accepts the women's superiority in 'wit' (meaning here, insight), and swears to eschew rhetoric and all such masculine attempts to impress:

> O, never will I trust to speeches penned,
> Nor to the motion of a schoolboy's tongue,
> Nor never come in visor to my friend,
> Nor woo in rhyme, like a blind harper's song.
> Taffeta phrases, silken terms precise,
> Three-piled hyperboles, spruce affectation,

Figures pedantical – these summer flies
Have blown me full of maggot ostentation.
I do forswear them, and I here protest
By this white glove – how white the hand, God knows –
Henceforth my wooing mind shall be expressed
In russet yeas and honest kersey noes.
And to begin, wench, so God help me, law!
My love to thee is sound, sans crack or flaw.

(5.2.402–16)

It's a perfect Shakespearean sonnet, all fourteen lines of it – Biron can't help himself, it seems. It's also a demonstration of the impossibility of speaking without rhetorical figures in the courtly mode, or indeed in any mode where one wants to communicate persuasively: 'russet yeas and honest kersey noes' is, ironically, a particularly fancy metaphor (referring to workmen's clothes) that supposedly expresses the preference for plainness. Rosaline, perhaps somewhat wearily, has to remind Biron that his apparent straight talk ('wench') is still tainted with fashionable French terms: 'Sans "sans", I pray you.'

Endings

Two events happen as the play draws to its end. First, as in the soon to be written *Midsummer Night's Dream*, the clowns put on a show for the gentlefolk. The theme of their show is the Nine Worthies, a parade of ancient heroes, meant as homage to the culture of their betters[8] – and indeed to the idea of 'fame' to which the lords aspired at the play's opening. Not surprisingly, it quickly descends into chaotic farce, with a threatened onstage fight between Costard and Don Armado, the rivals for Jaquenetta. Armado gets out of the fight, as farce's braggart soldier always does: this time by claiming he can't fight in his shirt because he isn't wearing one – a nice final touch of sophistry. Immediately following this is the other, completely unexpected event: the messenger Marcadé arrives from the French court with the news that the Princess's father is dead. He gives this news in two and a half lines of absolutely plain speech:

> MARCADÉ I am sorry, madam, for the news I bring
> Is heavy in my tongue. The King your father –
> PRINCESS Dead, for my life!
> MARCADÉ Even so. My tale is told.   (5.2.707–10)

The effect is completely to change the mood of the play: death has arrived at the comedy feast. Death, among other things, is a denial of linguistic power, of that which makes us human. The King tries to incorporate the event and control the outcome via an insensitive and obfuscating retreat to public rhetoric:

> The extreme parts of time extremely forms
> All causes to the purpose of his speed,
> And often at his very loose decides
> That which long process could not arbitrate.
> And though the mourning brow of progeny
> Forbid the smiling courtesy of love
> The holy suit which fain it would convince,
> Yet, since love's argument was first on foot,
> Let not the cloud of sorrow jostle it
> From what it purposed; since to wail friends lost
> Is not by much so wholesome-profitable
> As to rejoice at friends but newly found.
>
> (5.2.728–39)

As the Princess (now become Queen of France) replies, this is verbose and irrelevant jargon: 'I understand you not.' It is left to Biron, the most intelligent of the men, to try to rescue the situation: 'Honest plain words best pierce the ear of grief' – though it seems that, as usual, he is unable to stop talking once he has the floor: the speech segues quickly into an inappropriate and highly rhetorical declaration of love on behalf of all the men.

The women's response, led by their Queen, is that all the lords must wait for a year and a day before resuming their courtship. This is a more socially responsible version of the men's original plans to spend three years in seclusion – for a year, of course, is an appropriate period of mourning for the death of a king. Each of the men will in that time become more mature, and thus ready for the marriage that usually happens at the end of a comedy. Biron points out, metatheatrically, the bold nature of Shakespeare's suspended conclusion, which denies genre's complacency:

> Our wooing doth not end like an old play:
> Jack hath not Jill. These ladies' courtesy
> Might well have made our sport a comedy.
>
> (5.2.856–8)

Appropriately, it's the too-clever Biron who has the hardest task to fulfil in the year's delay: he must turn his eloquence to doing some good in the ordinary, inarticulate, pain-filled world:

> Visit the speechless sick, and still converse
> With groaning wretches; and your task shall be
> With all the fierce endeavour of your wit
> To enforce the painèd impotent to smile.
>
> (5.2.833–6)

He exclaims that this is an 'impossible' task, but Rosaline's final word of wisdom to her lover turns that perception on its head: offering a word to cheer others is more important than enjoying the sound of one's own witty remarks –

> A jest's prosperity lies in the ear
> Of him that hears it, never in the tongue
> Of him that makes it.

Love's Labour's Lost demonstrates the emotional limitations of a culture in which men are encouraged, via their education, to seek power through linguistic display. Rosaline's final speech insists on Christian humility and good deeds, rather than words. This being fulfilled, the courtiers can move on to a marriage of equals. It is an impressively serious and emotionally realistic conclusion for a comedy long thought of as essentially artificial.[9]

Shakespeare's one concession to a feel-good ending is the pair of songs performed in the little dialogue of Winter and Spring that the rustics and clowns offer as conclusion. Paradoxically, though appropriately (to those members of the audience who remain thoughtful), the spring song reminds us of the season's dark potential –

> Cuckoo, cuckoo! O word of fear,
> Unpleasing to a married ear!

And the winter song rejoices in the warmth of a humble fireside and the 'merry note' of the owl. The cycle of nature, we are reminded, is at least as complex as the structures created by nurture: gender, class, and education.

Romantic comedy

Love's Labour's Lost affectionately parodied the conventional trials of young lovers in the ancient genre of comedy – ending with surprising disappointment for the courtly characters; *Much Ado About Nothing, As You Like It,* and *Twelfth Night* together define what we now think of as the essence of 'romantic comedy', a genre still potent today. All three were written close together in the period 1599–1600. In this story-type the lovers do end up together, but only after trials that are not so much caused by external (material) problems as by internal psychological barriers. G. K. Hunter argues that *romance* is 'that comic form in which the complex of plot and character is read primarily in terms of character . . . [and] space is given for ethical [i.e. behavioural] choice and the contemplation of values'. He goes on to caution, however, that the notion of character 'development' is not an appropriate term, though it may help actors with their character's 'journey': 'We may say that we come to know such people, but we know them as people carried to their fates rather than people achieving them.'[1] *Romance* carries with it a suggestion of the mysterious actions of fate, as well as adventures in the world of the emotions. Place this in the standard form of comedy, with its guarantee of a happy ending for the young lovers and justice served out to any malign figures, and you have Shakespearean romantic comedy.

The narrative focus in these plays tends to be on the heady and confusing experience of being in love and the complexities created by gender roles and expectations. Witty language, which we saw anatomised in *Love's Labour's Lost*, is brought into play by the protagonists as a way of dealing with both the attraction and the fear of falling in love. Most revolutionary, in dramatic terms, is Shakespeare's decision to focus on the emotional life of the central female character, and make her story the play's driving force. In none of his earlier comedies does he really depart from the central focus on the male characters – though, as we have seen, there are moments of extraordinary eloquence for the female characters. The three romantic comedies discussed in this chapter provide three of the greatest roles for women in dramatic literature: Beatrice, Rosalind, and Viola *talk*, in their very different styles, as no dramatic heroine has talked before.

Romantic comedy is still the staple of the Hollywood comedy genre (farce remains a strong sub-group, of course, mostly in 'gross-out' movies). From the wonderful 1930s films featuring Fred Astaire and Ginger Rogers, which combined acerbic witty exchanges with sublimely sensual dance routines, to more quirky recent films such as *When Harry Met Sally* (Rob Reiner, 1989), or *My Best Friend's Wedding* (P. J. Hogan, 1997), where the romance has some unexpected turns and modern emotional complications, the audience expectation is that the two 'stars' will end up with each other, their charismatic performances often climaxing, just as in 1600, with a dance.

That *Twelfth Night* ends rather less euphorically is an important indicator that Shakespeare is moving on artistically, as I discuss towards the end of this chapter. In fact, the genre of romantic comedy operates with some assumptions which, even as he invented it, Shakespeare put into question. The first is heterosexuality, that is, the physical and emotional attraction of opposite genders: Jack and Jill. In two of these three plays Shakespeare consciously makes central to the plot the fact that his female protagonists are played by boys: Rosalind and Viola disguise their 'feminine' selves as boys in order, paradoxically, to continue their wooing of their surprisingly unobservant objects of desire. Beatrice, as I shall argue below, although she stays in female dress, positions herself in her society as an unfeminine woman – and thus, in fact, as much a disadvantaged 'outsider' as Viola or Rosalind. The supposedly easy and natural instant recognition of each other by a boy and a girl who are ready to fall in love – and all they have to do is overcome parental/social/financial barriers – is continually questioned by the events of these plays.

Secondly, as I have already indicated, Shakespeare chooses to make the woman's experience the emotional focus of the play: the audience learns of her feelings in a much more intimate way than they do those of the male characters, whose initial indications of being in love all tend to veer towards clichéd performances. It is this point that specifically differentiates Shakespearean romantic comedy from earlier popular 'romances', where the focus is usually on the hero who must try to attain the girl he has glimpsed or briefly met, and who likes to compose poetry about it to convince us of his great love. (This is the way *Romeo and Juliet* begins, before everything goes horribly wrong.) Shakespeare frequently draws on these old romances for his plots, but the single major change he makes is to put into the centre the experience of the female protagonist, the heroine, allowing us to see and hear her thoughts and emotional turmoil.

Much Ado About Nothing

Much Ado About Nothing is one of the few Shakespearean comedies set in a 'real' geographic location, in this case, Messina in Sicily. The audience is easily able to make connections between what they are seeing on stage and the conventions and behaviours of their own society: here are the local rich family and their servants, the townsfolk, and visiting soldiers. This is not, in short, a society in which a girl can disguise herself as a boy and fool everybody: it is too enclosed a community for that. Everyone knows everyone else's business, and if they don't, they make it up. Gossip is rife, much of it based on overhearing, or on 'noting' – watching and making a judgement that may well be false. The word *noting* (which puns on *nothing*) recurs throughout the play.

The play's realistic society is one in which the behaviour of the gentlefolk is ruled by strict conventions, especially regarding gender, but also regarding social hierarchy: there are two princes among the visitors, Don Pedro and his bastard brother, who are automatically deferred to by everyone. Or almost everyone: Beatrice and Benedick indicate their unconventionality by the freedom of their language in addressing those above them as equals. This does not go unnoticed by their friends, and much of *their* work in the play's process is to bring Beatrice and Benedick 'into a mountain of affection, th'one with th'other' (2.1.276–7), i.e. to cut them down to size so that they fit into 'normal' society as a married couple. In fact their final acknowledgement of love for each other and the necessity of marriage incorporates their rebellious energy into society, and thereby revitalises it. There's a sort of evolutionary instinct about this play; it celebrates the sexual success of the smartest.

In order to bring this about, the more conventional inhabitants of the play's society must engage in deception and gossip – which they are delighted to do, but the play also shows the danger of such behaviours in a community: Don John draws out its dark side using exactly the same mechanisms. The villain's destructive intentions are most powerful against the conventional couple, Claudio and Hero – we might argue, because they have no strong sense of themselves as individuals to protect them. Claudio is a young soldier who clearly hero-worships his leader, the good prince Don Pedro, and feels safest within the all-male military hierarchy. Hero is the only daughter of her widowed father; she is bound to consult and obey him in all matters. Beatrice by contrast is a 'poor relation', Leonato's niece, with no closer living relatives to try to keep her wit and outlandish behaviour under control. Of Benedick we know nothing, except that he is an upper-class soldier who likes to play the fool.

The conventional couple

Claudio and Hero's story embodies an older mythology of courtship and love than that of the defiant individuals Beatrice and Benedick. Its emotional and behavioural driver is Petrarchan (see chapter 3), and its underpinning ideology is patriarchal. Claudio begins by admiring Hero from afar (the conventional Petrarchan position) – as it were, on a pedestal, as an object whose worth can be judged by the eye:

> CLAUDIO Benedick, didst thou note the daughter of Signor Leonato?
> BENEDICK I noted her not, but I looked on her.
> CLAUDIO Is she not a modest young lady?
> . . . I pray thee, tell me truly how thou lik'st her?
> BENEDICK Would you buy her, that you enquire after her?
> CLAUDIO Can the world buy such a jewel?
> . . . In mine eye she is the sweetest lady that ever I looked on.
>
> (1.1.119–39)

'I can see yet without spectacles, and yet I see no such matter', says Benedick, attempting satirically to deflate Claudio's Petrarchan hyperbole. But 'noting' and 'looking' seem to be enough for Claudio; he doesn't need to get to know her personally, since, as the conversation proceeds (when Don Pedro joins it), all that really matters is that she is pretty, healthy, and wealthy (as Leonato's only heir). By the end of the play's opening scene he has happily agreed that Don Pedro, his social superior, will do the wooing for him in disguise, as long as in the end Leonato hands over Hero to him. Claudio's unthinking allegiance to social hierarchy makes him believe that his prince and commanding officer is a more persuasive wooer than he could be. The faults in this theory soon become apparent. Claudio is racked with jealousy and self-pity when he thinks that Don Pedro has stolen his prize:

> CLAUDIO Thus answer I in name of Benedick,
> But hear these ill news with the ears of Claudio:
> 'Tis certain so, the prince woos for himself,
> Friendship is constant in all other things
> Save in the office and affairs of love:
> Therefore all hearts in love use their own tongues.
> Let every eye negotiate for itself,
> And trust no agent: for beauty is a witch,
> Against whose charms faith melteth into blood:
>
> (2.1.128–36)

He consoles himself with a set of misanthropic generalisations (Friendship is . . . ; beauty is . . . ; trust no one), but appears unable to take them to heart, as he spends much of the rest of the play trusting everything but his own instincts and the object of his love. When the Prince clarifies the proxy wooing process, Claudio is struck dumb and Hero is silent. Beatrice, who fills the silence, underlines the bizarre fact that the audience have never heard Claudio and Hero speaking to each other. She commands the bewildered couple, 'Speak, count, 'tis your cue'; 'Speak, cousin, or (if you cannot) stop his mouth with a kiss, and let not him speak neither' (2.1.231, 235–6). The betrothal is performed with no communication between the couple, no attempt to get to know each other as young lovers. Hero in this scene is virtually a silent commodity, handed from her father to the Prince (the two male authority figures), and only then to Claudio.

In fact, Hero and Claudio's *only* face-to-face dialogue before the play's final scene is the explosion in 4.1, the aborted wedding scene, when Claudio accuses Hero of unchastity, something that he has been convinced of by (he believes) 'seeing' her at her bedroom window with a lover, an idea put into his head by Don John (the Vice-figure, who likes to ruin romances for his own entertainment). In this climactic scene Claudio complains vociferously about how Hero 'seemed' perfectly pure, until he was apparently shown otherwise:

> She's but the sign and semblance of her honour:
> Behold, how like a maid she blushes here!
> O, what authority and show of truth
> Can cunning sin cover itself withal!
> Comes not that blood, as modest evidence,
> To witness simple virtue? Would you not swear
> All you that see her, that she were a maid,
> By these exterior shows? But she is none:
> She knows the heat of a luxurious bed.
> Her blush is guiltiness, not modesty.
> . . . Out on thee seeming. I will write against it!
> You seem to me as Dian in her orb,
> As chaste as is the bud ere it be blown:
> But you are more intemperate in your blood,
> Than Venus, or those pampered animals,
> That rage in savage sensuality.
>   (4.1.28–37, 50–5)

These speeches rail obsessively against what Claudio believes to be the disjunction between Hero's appearance – 'signs' and 'shows' – and reality. But his 'reality' here is of course only another 'seeming', engineered by Don John.

Hero still barely utters a line to her betrothed. The authoritative males Leonato and Don Pedro do most of the responding; joined, eventually, by the Friar with his plan to pretend she is dead – the ultimate silence. Yet Hero has been merrily vocal in the scenes with her female friends: she does not lack linguistic capability, she is simply acculturated to being spoken for, or about, by men. In the second part of this scene, with Beatrice and Benedick alone on stage, Beatrice takes up the verbal cudgels for her silenced and slandered cousin, and for all women:

> BEATRICE Is a not approved in the height a villain, that hath slandered, scorned, dishonoured my kinswoman? Oh that I were a man! What, bear her in hand, until they come to take hands, and then with public accusation, uncovered slander, unmitigated rancour? Oh God that I were a man! I would eat his heart in the marketplace.   (4.1.291–5)

But, she concludes, 'I cannot be a man with wishing, therefore I will die a woman with grieving.' Ultimately she too, in this patriarchal society, must be dependent on a man to make right prevail. (Further aspects of this extraordinary scene, which also forms the climax of Beatrice and Benedick's courtship, will be discussed below.)

When Claudio finds out that Hero has indeed been slandered, he is still unable to move away linguistically from his cultural attitude of judging by appearances:

> Sweet Hero, now thy *image* doth *appear*
> In the rare *semblance* that I loved it first.   (5.1.220–1, italics added)

The unconscious irony with which he speaks here is continued visually, when he performs his rite of atonement – parading as a heartbroken lover around 'Hero's monument' with poetry and music. The pedestal is now empty (though, ghoulishly, he thinks her body is safely inside the monument). And of course he accepts a 'new' wife at Leonato's hands without even seeing her face – much less speaking to her. In his terms Claudio is doing the honourable thing: for the audience, he seems not to have learnt anything at all, as he stays firmly within the conventional model of gender and social relations – in which model you can *perform* 'being a lover' by using the courtly love tropes of admiration from a safe distance. Their final brief exchange is bleak:

> HERO And when I lived I was your other wife;
> And when you loved you were my other husband.
> CLAUDIO Another Hero?
> HERO Nothing certainer.
> One Hero died defiled, but I do live,
> And surely as I live, I am a maid.   (5.4.60–4)

The audience may well wonder what the future of this barely communicating couple will be.

The 'merry war' of Beatrice and Benedick

No such wondering need occur with the play's other romantic couple, Beatrice and Benedick – the couple who talk, and bicker, endlessly, thus displaying for each other their intellects, their energy, and their compatibility. At all points, we see their linguistic vitality, which is particularly shown up by contrast with the 'ordinary' folk amongst whom they live. Beatrice makes her difference clear very early in the play, about 25 lines in:

> BEATRICE I pray you, is Signor Mountanto returned from the wars or no?
> MESSENGER I know none of that name, lady, there was none such in the army of any sort.   (1.1.23–5)

The hapless messenger is literally unable to understand her question. Her follow-up sally – 'I pray you, how many hath he killed and eaten in these wars? But how many hath he killed? – for indeed I promised to eat all of his killing' – is equally bizarre, and Leonato has to intervene with 'You must not, sir, mistake my niece: there is a kind of merry war betwixt Signor Benedick and her: they never meet but there's a skirmish of wit between them.' His use of military metaphors here is significant: it suggests that Beatrice thinks (and behaves) in an unfeminine, masculine way. Throughout the play Beatrice's language is striking: often approaching the indecorous, it draws attention to her in a way not dissimilar to the clown's knowing appeal via wit to the audience, both onstage and offstage. Benedick's verbal riffs have exactly the same function: they are, in fact, a pair of outsiders to conventional behaviour, a pair of clowns.

This function is made quite clear to the audience in the exchange of quips and insults that they throw at each other when they meet in the play. It is the highlight of the play's opening scene: the ordinary folk (ourselves included) watch as though they are at a masters' tennis-match – not a love-match, rather one that goes all the way to deuce (the Devil) before Benedick hits the winning ace. It begins thus, with arresting indecorum:

> BEATRICE I wonder that you will still be talking, Signor Benedick, nobody marks you.
> BENEDICK What, my dear Lady Disdain! Are you yet living?
> BEATRICE Is it possible Disdain should die while she hath such meet food to feed it, as Signor Benedick? Courtesy itself must convert to Disdain, if you come in her presence.

> BENEDICK Then is Courtesy a turncoat. But it is certain I am loved of
> all ladies, only you excepted; and I would I could find in my heart that
> I had not a hard heart, for truly I love none.   (1.1.86–94)

Something that would have been clear to the play's first audience is that
both speakers use the terms of Petrarchan poetic discourse as contemptuous
brickbats: 'Lady Disdain', 'Courtesy'. The latter in particular is an attitude that
neither is the least bit interested in – they'd rather be trading insults. Although
this might suggest that Beatrice is a shrew (compare the first meeting between
Katherina and Petruchio), Benedick is no Petruchio, no tamer – he has neither
the proprietorial nor the bullying attitude, but simply hits the winning shot in
this opening rally by announcing 'I have done' – for the time being.

Many actresses playing Beatrice have picked up on the clue given in the last
line of this exchange, 'I know you of old', to build a back-story for Beatrice that
includes a previous relationship with Benedick; and at a rather tense moment
in 2.1's conversation with Don Pedro, she admits that Benedick 'once before
won [my heart] of me, with false dice' (2.1.212). This certainly suggests that the
actors of Beatrice and Benedick should be cast as older than the naïve Claudio
and Hero, and that they do know something about love and its dangers. What
the conversation also confirms is that Beatrice is no shrew, whatever Benedick
may claim to think: there is an awkward, poignant moment in which Don
Pedro is so attracted by her vitality that he impulsively proposes to her:

> DON PEDRO Will you have me, lady?
> BEATRICE No, my lord, unless I might have another for working days,
>   your grace is too costly to wear every day: but I beseech your grace
>   pardon me, I was born to speak all mirth and no matter.
> DON PEDRO Your silence most offends me, and to be merry best
>   becomes you, for out a question, you were born in a merry hour.
> BEATRICE No, sure, my lord, my mother cried; but then there was a
>   star danced, and under that was I born.   (2.1.248–55)

Beatrice's embarrassed response (to an offer brought about by her indecorous
wit) is of course correct – Don Pedro cannot marry a fatherless commoner.
But his perception of her 'pleasant-spirited' nature (and the fact that he, unlike
Claudio, thinks female silence 'offends') matches her own self-assessment –
'born to speak all mirth and no matter', perhaps, but also born under a dancing
star.

Don Pedro, possibly self-protectively, remarks to his companions, 'She were
an excellent wife for Benedick', and by the end of this scene, the plot to 'bring
Signor Benedick and the Lady Beatrice into a mountain of affection, th'one

with th'other' is agreed on. Both onstage and offstage audiences have heard them declare that they won't marry – since, implicitly, that would force them to behave 'normally', to submit to the patriarchal myth and deny their individuality. But as clown-like characters with an overweening opinion of themselves, they are set up for the fall which we know is inevitable – what we might call the fall from an illusion of freedom into the bonds of a genre that insists on ending in marriages.

Both 'gulling' scenes, in which the ordinary folk conspire to trick the too-clever ones, are comedic. But there is a difference in style between them; Shakespeare does not simply repeat the joke. In the simplest technical terms, Benedick's scene is almost entirely in prose, Beatrice's is entirely in blank verse, and this stylistic difference dictates an emotional contrast.

Benedick is given plenty of opportunities for clowning in his scene (2.3). He begins by chatting to the audience in a long stand-up routine, which starts with a complaint about Claudio's transformation into a conventional lover, and ends by fantasising about his own ideal woman, a rather more realistic figure:

> Rich she shall be, that's certain: wise, or I'll none: virtuous, or I'll never cheapen her: fair, or I'll never look on her: mild, or come not near me: noble, or not I for an angel: of good discourse, an excellent musician – and her hair shall be of what colour it please God.   (2.3.23–7)

As he then hides while trying to overhear the conversation of Claudio, Don Pedro, and Leonato, the actor of Benedick has multiple opportunities for physical gags and pratfalls. The scene is finally framed with another stand-up monologue in which this clownish figure, with a new role as a lover, shares his justification for the about-face with the audience:

> This can be no trick, the conference was sadly borne, they have the truth of this from Hero, they seem to pity the lady: it seems her affections have their full bent: love me? Why, it must be requited: I hear how I am censured, they say I will bear myself proudly, if I perceive the love come from her: they say too, that she will rather die than give any sign of affection: I did never think to marry, I must not seem proud, happy are they that hear their detractions, and can put them to mending: they say the lady is fair, 'tis a truth, I can bear them witness: and virtuous, 'tis so, I cannot reprove it: and wise, but for loving me: by my troth it is no addition to her wit, nor no great argument of her folly, for I will be horribly in love with her: I may chance have some odd quirks and remnants of wit broken on me, because I have railed so long against marriage: but doth not the appetite alter? A man loves the meat in his

> youth, that he cannot endure in his age. Shall quips and sentences, and
> these paper bullets of the brain awe a man from the career of his
> humour? No, the world must be peopled. When I said I would die a
> bachelor, I did not think I should live till I were married.   (2.3.181–98)

The audience sees how the amateur theatrical performance of his friends has
called Benedick into a new understanding of himself and the world. This understanding does not deprive him of his fertile wit and verbal energy, but rather
finds a productive role for them: the world must, after all, 'be peopled', and
why not by witty, amusing characters?

Beatrice by contrast is given much less opportunity for humour in her gulling
scene (3.1), though she too must hide and react to what she hears. The scene's
blank verse creates a more serious mood than the prose of Benedick's scene, and
Beatrice is in fact silent until her final soliloquy – she has no interjections, as
Benedick has. When she does speak it is the form of the last ten lines of a Shakespearean sonnet, with its typical complex rhyme scheme and unconventional
psychological revelations.

> What fire is in mine ears? Can this be true?
>   Stand I condemned for pride and scorn so much?
> Contempt, farewell, and maiden pride, adieu,
>   No glory lives behind the back of such.
> And, Benedick, love on, I will requite thee,
>   Taming my wild heart to thy loving hand:
> If thou dost love, my kindness shall incite thee
>   To bind our loves up in a holy band,
> For others say thou dost deserve, and I
>   Believe it better than reportingly.   (3.1.107–16)

The speech is addressed to her inner self and the absent Benedick, not the
audience: we are privileged overhearers of her emotional life – just as we sometimes think ourselves when we read Shakespeare's own extraordinary sequence
of sonnets.

The final part of the church scene (4.1) eventually enables the couple to show
their real feelings for each other – but only after the distressing scene of the
public breakdown of the wedding between Claudio and Hero, where he speaks
so vilely to her that she is left for dead. It is this failure of conventional structures
that (appropriately) brings together the unconventional lovers. When Beatrice
and Benedick are finally left alone on stage – and we, and Benedick, note that she
has been weeping 'all this while', we hear a dialogue that is at once an eloquent
love scene and a spelling-out of the unavoidable social imperatives of gender,
as they were then conceived: men must fight, and women must weep. Beatrice's

shocking demand of Benedick that he prove his love for her by killing Claudio is a desperate acknowledgement of the power of this ideology, in particular the insidious notion of honour.

Fortunately the conventions of the comedy genre ensure that the truth is revealed before Benedick fights Claudio (though not before he has challenged him, thus showing his good faith to Beatrice). The warm and witty conversation of the now acknowledged lovers in 5.2 reassures us that they have not succumbed to the old model of distant fantasising, despite occasional half-hearted attempts at poetry and song by Benedick, and the final scene's revelation of 'halting sonnets' by both of them. They represent a new style of adult, self-confident lovers who enjoy each other's company. 'Thou and I are too wise to woo peaceably', they acknowledge (5.2.54). Their final encounter at the play's end unites both aspects of the roles that these two characters have played: as clown-like 'entertainers' on the periphery of conventional society, and as role-models for a modern version of romance that signals mutual desire through witty banter. With Benedick's 'Peace, I will stop your mouth', the audience finally get the kiss they have been waiting for. But its connotation is ambiguous: Beatrice's mouth is literally stopped – she doesn't say a word after this. Benedick talks on to the play's end, very much the new dominant male, the representative of the next generation: ordering dancing (despite Leonato's objection), impertinently telling the Prince 'Get thee a wife', and saying that he (not Don Pedro) will devise 'brave punishments' for Don John.

The play's little community may have learnt something about the dangerous power of gossip and rumour, but nothing has really changed, and at the end it looks forward to replicating itself in the next generation. *Much Ado* may appear transgressive, even revolutionary, in its new model of gender relations, but in the end it reincorporates the energies of the transgressive couple into its social order. This is symbolised by the final dance whose purpose is, Benedick says, to 'lighten our own hearts and our wives' heels' – a strong contrast with the tensions of the deceptive masked dance of the play's opening movement (2.1), in which all relationships were tainted by disguise.

Three clowns

Much Ado has a role for the company's professional clown: the town constable Dogberry, probably written for Will Kemp (who left the Chamberlain's Men in 1599). He doesn't appear until the middle of the play, 3.3; the 'law' isn't needed until then. I have suggested that Beatrice and Benedick up to this point are the play's 'clowns' – and, indeed, they are seen as such by the other characters in the community. Benedick is particularly affronted that he should be labelled as 'the prince's jester' or 'the prince's fool' (2.1.103, 155), Beatrice that she should be accused of having her 'good wit out of *The Hundred Merry Tales*' (2.1.96). Both are thus associated with professional fools, and they have ambivalent attitudes to this – it distinguishes them, gives them a social role, yet at the same time prevents their complete absorption into genteel society. It also operates as their safeguard against unwilling assimilation.

Each of them in the play's early scenes indulges in outlandish language. Beatrice's aggressive opening sallies in 1.1 – 'how many hath he killed and eaten?' etc.; her extravagant speeches on the desirability of men with and without beards and on the analogies between 'wooing, wedding, and repenting' and various dances (2.1): all claim the right to be heard that the professional wit claims (and that the quiet young woman Hero never claims). It seems entirely appropriate that her joke about her meeting with St Peter has him showing her 'where the bachelors sit, and there live we as merry as the day is long' (2.1.37). Beatrice claims to prefer the status and freedom of a bachelor (not the female 'spinster') – which is of course exactly what Benedick also claims. (Shakespearean clowns are rarely married; if they are, it is likely not to last – 'but two months victualled', as Jaques says of Touchstone's inappropriate marriage in *As You Like It*.)

Benedick's clown-like over-the-top utterances are more loquacious: they come from one who is culturally used to taking centre-stage. A good example is his performance of exaggerated horror when Beatrice comes on stage in 2.1, the conclusion of an even longer speech complaining about her treatment of him:

> Will your grace command me any service to the world's end? I will go on the slightest errand now to the Antipodes that you can devise to send me on: I will fetch you a tooth-picker now from the furthest inch of Asia: bring you the length of Prester John's foot: fetch you a hair off the Great Cham's beard: do you any embassage to the Pygmies, rather than hold three words conference with this Harpy. (2.1.199–204)

'Antipodes', 'the great Cham', 'Prester John' (and does he really mean 'foot' or is there a suggestive pause here?): all are exotic terms that evoke laughter in association with the absurd errands that Benedick proposes. Don Pedro's response to his desperate 'You have no employment for me?' – 'None but to desire your good company' – confirms Benedick's role as 'the prince's jester' (2.1.103).

After the virtuoso comic performance that 2.3 (the gulling scene) offers to the actor playing Benedick, his next appearance, in 3.2, encourages him to *look* like a clown: his companions tease him about his random mix of fashion styles, his new haircut, and general foppish air. In fact he is briefly trying to ape the style of the narcissistic courtly lover in optimistic mode, to behave as literary tradition dictates. Although he soon gives this up, he is still treated as the clown when he comes to challenge Claudio in 5.1: 'We have been up and down to seek thee, for we are high proof melancholy, and would fain have it beaten away, wilt thou use thy wit?', says Claudio (5.1.118–21). But Benedick maintains his dignity and his newfound masculinity, and his challenge is eventually taken seriously. Appropriately, Dogberry arrives on the scene with the news of Hero's innocence five lines after Benedick has swept offstage. The true professional clown takes over, as he did in his wonderful language-mangling arrival in 3.3 – and, paradoxically (against all reason), he brings about the triumph of truth. This says something about the essentially benign world of the genre of comedy; it is ultimately *not* dependent on human reason or the careful and legally accurate use of language. Dogberry shares with Beatrice and Benedick a rich fund of verbal energy – and that energy, used with confidence towards good ends, even if it's a somewhat blunt instrument, will conquer. (It's worth noting that the villain Don John at his first introduction insists that he is 'not of many words' (1.1.116).) Dogberry's free-associating verbal extravaganzas finally take him out of the play in comic triumph, confident that his role in society – whether as constable or clown – is both important and beneficent:

> God keep your worship, I wish your worship well, God restore you to health, I humbly give you leave to depart, and if a merry meeting may be wished, God prohibit it: come, neighbour.   (5.1.286–9)

As You Like It

Unlike the realistic community of *Much Ado*'s Messina, *As You Like It* is structured round a symbolic contrast familiar to Elizabethan audiences: the court and the country. This contrast was the mainstay of one of the most popular of Elizabethan literary genres, the pastoral. It was to be found in sonnets and songs (including many madrigals), in verse dialogues or eclogues, including an influential work by the major non-dramatic poet of the period, Edmund Spenser (*The Shephearde's Calender*, 1579), and in novels such as Thomas Lodge's *Rosalynde* (1590) on which Shakespeare based his play. It contrasted the lives of idealised shepherds and shepherdesses with the behaviour of the educated men and women of the court. Each of these claimed to envy the life of the other – natural simplicity or courtly sophistication.

Writing the play in 1599, Shakespeare took advantage of his audience's familiarity with this fashion. But he took it into areas that they could not have predicted, largely by layering it with his own interests in the politics of gender, a field that he had begun exploring in the comedies written up to this point. *As You Like It* is more famous, now, for the charismatic role of the cross-dressed Rosalind than for its satire of pastoral conventions. And if we can argue that Shakespeare is staging the controlling mechanisms of the social construction of gender in *Much Ado About Nothing*, then we can call *As You Like It* a full-scale deconstruction of those mechanisms. By having Rosalind self-consciously and pleasurably play the girl playing the boy playing the girl – and originally, it was of course a boy actor playing the girl Rosalind – Shakespeare stages the *fluidity* of gender-construction for our instruction and delight.[2]

Just as Beatrice is on the periphery of Leonato's household, and – importantly – fatherless, so is Rosalind, the heroine of *As You Like It*, cousin and best friend of the more conventional young woman, Celia. Once again, this marginal position enables behaviour that would not be possible for the conventional girl. But then there's a surprising development. At the end of Act 1, when Rosalind has been banished simply for being her exiled father's daughter, Celia declares that she will not play the obedient daughter, but will run away with Rosalind, 'To liberty, and not to banishment.' Thus, even though much of the rest of the play concerns the cross-dressed Rosalind's doubly disguised wooing of Orlando, there is also a deployment of the theme of sisterhood – the strong and mutually supportive bonds, going back to childhood, between two very different adult women. Throughout the play Celia (also, let us remember, a cross-dressed boy actor originally) functions in this sisterly role as well as in the role of conventional feminine and genteel young woman who attempts to rein in the excesses of Rosalind's cross-dressed indecorum.

Pastoral ideal vs. political violence

The play begins with a quarrel between two brothers – Oliver, the elder brother who has claimed all their father's estate, and Orlando, the dispossessed youngest son. It begins, that is, with the typical masculine concerns of the folk-tale narrative – 'There comes an old man and his three sons', as Le Beau puts it (1.2.93).[3] The whole of Act 1 is set in this world of male power and the violence associated with it: Orlando's attack on his brother, out of frustrated rage, a mere forty lines into the play; his bout with the famously violent Charles the wrestler in 1.2 (when he unexpectedly wins this, there is the first glimmer of reassurance for the audience that the traditional folk-tale success of the youngest son will indeed come about); finally, the tyrannical banishment of Rosalind by Duke Frederick.

When Rosalind and Celia decide to leave this oppressive male-dominated environment and flee to the Forest of Arden, they make significant decisions about their costumes, and thus their public identities. Rosalind opts for the appearance of masculinity, a swashbuckling hunter with echoes of commedia's Capitano (with *two* phallic weapons):

> ROSALIND Were it not better,
> Because that I am more than common tall,
> That I did suit me all points like a man,
> A gallant curtal-axe upon my thigh,
> A boar-spear in my hand, and in my heart
> Lie there what hidden woman's fear there will,
> We'll have a swashing and a martial outside,
> As many other mannish cowards have
> That do outface it with their semblances.
>
> (1.3.104–12)

Celia decides to put herself 'in poor and mean attire, / And with a kind of umber smirch [her] face' – that is, to take a major drop in class status, though retaining the appearance of a woman (and thus also the vulnerability of her gender, unlike Rosalind). These decisions involve re-namings; the young women will no longer bear the names that their godparents gave them at their church christening, but make their own decisions about who they are:

> CELIA What shall I call thee when thou art a man?
> ROSALIND I'll have no worse a name than Jove's own page,
> And therefore look you call me 'Ganymede'.
> But what will you be called?
> CELIA Something that hath a reference to my state:
> No longer 'Celia' but 'Aliena'. (1.3.113–18)

Both names are easily decodable by the audience. Ganymede is the young male lover of the pagan god Jove, and slang for homosexual toy-boy in Elizabethan English. Aliena (a made-up name) refers to Celia's newly outcast state. Celia's excited couplet at the end of Act 1 –

> Now go we in content,
> To liberty, and not to banishment.

– has striking connotations: like their re-naming of themselves, the word 'banishment' can be re-interpreted as that most dangerous of political cries, 'Liberty!'

Act 2 opens strangely, however: we are transported to Arden, where we see the banished Duke Senior (Rosalind's father) and his court-in-exile: all men. Will this world be any different for the fleeing girls? From the Duke we hear a well-rehearsed set-piece about the spiritual goods of living close to nature (one of the myths of the pastoral genre, especially in its classical Latin form):

> Now, my co-mates and brothers in exile,
> Hath not old custom made this life more sweet
> Than that of painted pomp? Are not these woods
> More free from peril than the envious court?
> . . . Sweet are the uses of adversity
> Which like the toad, ugly and venomous,
> Wears yet a precious jewel in his head,
> And this our life exempt from public haunt,
> Finds tongues in trees, books in the running brooks,
> Sermons in stones, and good in everything.
>
> (2.1.1–17)

Indeed, as Amiens comments, perhaps with some irony,

> I would not change it. Happy is your grace,
> That can translate the stubbornness of fortune
> Into so quiet and so sweet a style.
>
> (2.1.18–20)

But the very next moment Duke Senior is proposing that they go off to hunt deer for food. He is not unaware of this contradiction in the idyllic lifestyle that he has just described: that the deer, 'the poor dappled fools, / Being native burghers of this desert city', should be 'gored'. And he has a philosopher amongst the court-in-exile, 'the melancholy Jaques', who has forcefully pointed out the ethical contradictions of the imposition of their lifestyle on the forest, making a significant connection between the actions that we saw in Act 1 and those that we may see of this group of men: Jaques, says the First Lord,

> swears you do more usurp
> Than doth your brother that hath banished you.
> . . . Thus most invectively he pierceth through
> The body of country, city, court,
> Yea, and of this our life, swearing that we
> Are mere usurpers, tyrants, and what's worse,
> To fright the animals and to kill them up
> In their assigned and native dwelling-place.
>
> (2.1.27–8, 58–63)

According to Jaques, there seems to be no way that human beings can avoid being violent, whether in 'country, city, court'. As the play then veers briefly back to Duke Frederick and his bullying, and Oliver and his murderous plans for Orlando, the connection is kept clear in the audience's mind. It is a highly significant moment, then, when in 2.4 Rosalind and Celia first appear in the forest, disguised, and in conversation with a shepherd decide to set themselves up as cottagers and keepers of sheep. Shepherding is a much less violent occupation than hunting; it is associated with female-oriented occupations such as spinning and weaving. From this point onwards Rosalind dresses as a 'shepherd', without the martial weaponry; and we understand that Celia has made a virtue out of her class transition: she has become a landholder, a businesswoman in fact – and the kindly face of nascent capitalism. She says to Corin, 'we will mend thy wages. I like this place / And willingly could waste my time in it' (2.4.87–8). As the owner of the business and employer of Corin, she of course won't have to labour herself. Celia has established a realistic – albeit utopian – embodiment of the pastoral literary fantasy.

To underline this political argument, the play reverts twice more to scenes of male violence: first, briefly, when Orlando comes upon Duke Senior and his men feasting, and demands food with drawn sword (2.7). He is soon disabused of the necessity for this, and we next see him gently carrying on stage his old servant Adam and feeding him – a striking image of feminine nurturing: 'like a doe', he says, 'I go to find my fawn / And give it food' (2.7.128–9). Despite the apparent preference for non-violent ways, however, amongst the court-in-exile, there is a short late scene (4.2, often cut, though it is integral) which celebrates the bloody killing of deer in the hunt. The triumphant hunting song is ambivalent: its chorus, 'The horn, the horn, the lusty horn, / Is not a thing to laugh to scorn' refers both to the triumphal headdress of the hunter, and to the ever-present possibility of the cuckold's horns. Male dominance of the social order is fragile, always vulnerable to the struggle for supremacy amongst men.

As a postscript to this aspect of the play's narrative, it is worth noting that very late in the play the now repentant Oliver comes on (and immediately falls in love with Celia, and she with him). His brother Orlando, he reports, has saved him, destitute and alone, from being eaten by a lioness, when he might have left him to die:

> But kindness, nobler ever than revenge,
> And nature, stronger than his just occasion,
> Made him give battle to the lioness,
> Who quickly fell before him.   (4.3.123–6)

Orlando has used his masculine strength in a proper way, to help the oppressed, and not to wreak revenge for his brother's past injustices. He will make a good husband and leader of the community in the restorations that the play's finale foreshadows.

Rosalind's cross-dressing: release into language

Rosalind not only changes in appearance, from court lady to hunter to shepherd boy, she also changes her behaviour, from being the less talkative and slightly more subdued of the two girls in Act 1 (Celia, after all, is in her own home, Rosalind is a guest and the daughter of the exiled Duke), to playing the eloquently witty and outrageously flirtatious Ganymede for the remaining four acts of the play. We might well infer that her 'true self' has been released by the change of costume, gender, and situation. Or we might simply say that she is seizing an opportunity, in the temporary space of liberty that is the Forest of Arden, to talk and talk, and take the lead in a courtship situation. For the first time in her life, she is unconstrained by conventional notions of femininity. Arguably, the original theatre audience was observing, perhaps for the first time, the spectacle of a woman dominating the conversation but divorced from the notion that this is 'shrewish' behaviour.

Rosalind talks mainly in prose, not blank verse (so, largely, does Beatrice). Prose allows for fluid, complex, unpredictable verbal play, because it's not constrained by the traditions of rhetoric that accompany blank verse. In fact, Rosalind's only substantial blank verse speech is in 3.5, to Phebe, where she needs to play the authoritative male – and seems to revel in it:

> And why, I pray you? Who might be your mother
> That you insult, exult, and all at once
> Over the wretched? What, though you have no beauty,
> As, by my faith, I see no more in you
> Than without candle may go dark to bed,
> Must you be therefore proud and pitiless?
> ... 'Tis not your inky brows, your black silk hair,
> Your bugle eyeballs, nor your cheek of cream
> That can entame my spirits to your worship.
> ... But, mistress, know yourself. Down on your knees,
> And thank heaven, fasting, for a good man's love;
> For I must tell you friendly in your ear,
> Sell when you can: you are not for all markets.
>
> (3.6.34–60)

Amusingly, even this schoolmasterly bluntness has no power over the besotted Phebe, rapt as she is in the conventions of courtly love: 'Sweet youth, I pray you chide a year together; / I had rather hear you chide than this man woo', she replies (3.6.64–5).

Rosalind's wooing scenes with Orlando are the most remarkable of her performances as the androgynous Ganymede. They operate through a free-wheeling, witty, erudite satirisation and deconstruction of Petrarchanism. The conventions of courtly love drive romantic relationships in popular literature; they are reliably productive of sighs, weeping, irrationality, obsession – everything that we see young Silvius suffering for the unrequited love of Phebe; and everything that, thankfully, Orlando is not. He does *not* have a lean cheek, neglected beard, ungartered hose, untied shoes (3.2). Orlando, that is, whatever his failings as a poet – we have heard his excruciating verses to Rosalind ('tedious homilies', she says) – is a healthy young man driven by desire to do *something* to sublimate his passion. Thus, he is a ready collaborator with Rosalind's plan to pretend to be his lady-love and thereby 'cure' him of his passion. Although he claims, 'I would not be cured, youth', by the end of this scene he has given in to Rosalind's charismatic insistence on offering him some substitute for his absent beloved. To see how this has come about we need to go back earlier into the scene, before Orlando even arrives.

In the long opening discussion between Rosalind and Celia we see and hear a Rosalind who is herself just as hyperactively in love as Orlando is. She doesn't have the courtly lover's option of writing poems and 'abusing' trees; all she can do is talk to – or at – her best friend. The energy of her speech, its piled-up unanswered questions, its outlandish metaphors, explodes like a fireworks show:

> ROSALIND Good my complexion, dost thou think, though I am
> caparisoned like a man, I have a doublet and hose in my disposition?
> One inch of delay more is a South Sea of discovery. I prithee tell me
> who is it – quickly, and speak apace. I would thou couldst stammer
> that thou might'st pour this concealed man out of thy mouth as wine
> comes out of a narrow-mouthed bottle: either too much at once or
> none at all. I prithee take the cork out of thy mouth that I may drink
> thy tidings.   (3.3.162–9)

Celia can barely get a word in, but finally assures Rosalind of what she wanted to hear, and receives another manic response:

> ROSALIND Alas the day, what shall I do with my doublet and hose?
> What did he when thou saw'st him? What said he? How looked he?
> Wherein went he? What makes he here? Did he ask for me? Where
> remains he? How parted he with thee, and when shalt thou see him
> again? Answer me in one word.   (3.3.181–8)

This energy impels into her hailing Orlando 'like a saucy lackey', and beginning the first long witty exchange with him. It seemingly doesn't actually matter what they are talking about, just that they should display to each other their vitality, their wit, their suitability to be a couple. (It is no wonder that Orlando doesn't recognise her – both were virtually speechless in their meeting in Act 1.) They have none of the back-story of Beatrice and Benedick, so there is no spikiness in their exchange, just delight. For Orlando, someone to talk to, at last! – and clearly more fun than the solemn rhetoric of the Duke in exile and the melancholy Jaques (his only conversation with Jaques is in lines 214–49 of this scene; they part by mutual agreement).

Their second courtship scene, 4.1 – this time introduced by a slightly edgy conversation between Jaques and Rosalind – while still driven by the same verbal energy, is more fraught. Rosalind complains of Orlando's lateness; he offers to kiss her (she evades this alarming move with more words); he complains of continuing frustration and threatens to 'die' like a true Petrarchan. This produces another extraordinary speech from Rosalind, critiquing the whole literary tradition of courtly love for its ignorance of emotional realism:

> No, faith, die by attorney. The poor world is almost six thousand years old and in all this time there was not any man died in his own person, videlicet [namely], in a love-cause. Troilus had his brains dashed out with a Grecian club, yet he did what he could to die before, and he is one of the patterns of love; Leander, he would have lived many a fair year though Hero had turned nun, if it had not been for a hot midsummer night, for, good youth, he went but forth to wash him in the Hellespont and, being taken with the cramp, was drowned, and the foolish chroniclers of that age found it was Hero of Sestos. But these are all lies: men have died from time to time – and worms have eaten them – but not for love.   (4.1.75–85)

Rosalind's verbal display regains her the advantage. She uses it to demand that Celia 'marry' them, and, overcoming Celia's objection that she 'cannot say the words' (Celia is always conscious of the rules of femininity), Rosalind brings about a most audacious theatrical moment. She instructs Celia in the words to be spoken by the priest in the church service – and as if that wasn't sacrilegious enough, she then ensures that both she and Orlando speak the lines that constitute a legal marriage in Elizabethan society:

> ROSALIND ... you must say, 'I take thee, Rosalind, for wife.'
> ORLANDO I take thee, Rosalind, for wife.
> ROSALIND I might ask you for your commission; but I do take thee, Orlando, for my husband.   (4.1.108–12)

Excited, perhaps slightly embarrassed banter follows this moment (often the actors do kiss at this point, just as in most weddings); and when Orlando extricates himself claiming an appointment with the Duke, Rosalind again expresses in charged prose to her confidante, the outraged Celia, the depth of her passion: 'O coz, coz, coz, my pretty little coz, that thou didst know how many fathom deep I am in love!' (4.1.165–6).

Finally, there comes a point when Orlando (now actually wounded in the fight with the lioness, *not* metaphorically 'wounded' by love) says, 'I can live no longer by thinking' – or imagining. Rosalind offers to bring the play's 'idle talking' to an end, and to do so with the assistance of 'magic' that the audience knows to be theatrical: to 'set [Rosalind] before your eyes . . . human as she is'. It is time, that is, for the action that only she can bring about, the revelation of truth. We might say that since she's been liberated into eloquent, daring speech, she has recognised her own power, her 'unfeminine' energy that can be put to good use in a world where – at least temporarily – patriarchal power doesn't entirely rule.

There is a poignant but inevitable irony to this conclusion. Comedy, while delighting in the events of a briefly topsy-turvy world, is ultimately conservative: its mission is to revitalise the social status quo by reincorporating the energies of the 'outlandish', through the institution of marriage in particular. As soon as she reappears in female costume, and makes the ritual re-assignment of herself to her astonished father and husband, Rosalind is silent (like Beatrice) until the play finishes. But Shakespeare has one more trick up his theatrical sleeve. There is the traditional dance, commanded by the now restored Duke Senior. It is followed by Rosalind's extraordinary, unexpected, and indecorous epilogue:

> It is not the fashion to see the lady the Epilogue; but it is no more unhandsome than to see the lord the Prologue . . . My way is to conjure you, and I'll begin with the women. I charge you, O women, for the love you bear to men, to like as much of this play as please you. – And I charge you, O men, for the love you bear to women – as I perceive by your simpering none of you hates them – that between you and the women the play may please. If I were a woman, I would kiss as many of you as had beards that pleased me, complexions that liked me, and breaths that I defied not. And I am sure as many as have good beards, or good faces, or sweet breaths will, for my kind offer, when I make curtsey, bid me farewell.

Although Shakespearean epilogues normally act as a 'bridge' for the audience back to the real world, this one actually takes us back into the world of the play, where gender is fluid and undetermined, dependent only on the choice of the performer. It leaves the audience delightfully confused, sure of only one thing: the charismatic presence of the actor playing Rosalind.

Clowns

As well as Rosalind's freewheeling wit and game-playing, the play offers a role for the traditional Elizabethan clown – in this case, Touchstone, the Duke's jester who prefers to take his chance with the runaway girls rather than stay with the bullying Duke Frederick. Touchstone thus finds himself, to his astonishment, in the Forest of Arden, where he can encounter the other sort of Elizabethan 'clown', the unsophisticated rustic (he insists on the point by addressing Corin as 'clown' in 2.4, and saying of William, Audrey's suitor, in 5.1, 'It is meat and drink to me to see a clown'). This offers an opportunity to test the conventional court/country oppositions of pastoral. In the discussion between Touchstone and Corin, the old shepherd, in 3.2, Corin's account of the realities of country life wins hands down over Touchstone's 'courtly wit', which is mostly based on smart but meaningless puns.

Touchstone, moreover, falls in love with a country wench, Audrey, who is the very opposite of 'poetical' – she doesn't even know what the word means: 'Is it honest in deed and word? Is it a true thing?' (3.3). Of course not! As Touchstone admits, 'the truest poetry is the most feigning', especially where lovers are concerned. This short excursus into literary theory might resonate with some members of the audience, who could reflect, briefly, that they are at that very moment subject to the 'feigning' power of Shakespeare's language, the 'feigning' power of actors, and the curious emotional truth that this situation can create.

The one character who has an intellectual response to Touchstone and his professional role is the melancholy satirist Jaques. He is watching – like the audience – the scene between Audrey and Touchstone just quoted, and he intervenes to delay this socially inappropriate marriage based on nothing more than lust. But throughout the play he is curiously fascinated by Touchstone. He reports in 2.7 with great excitement,

> A fool, a fool: I met a fool i'th'forest,
> A motley fool – a miserable world –
> As I do live by food, I met a fool
> Who laid him down and basked him in the sun,
> And railed on Lady Fortune in good terms,
> In good set terms, and yet a motley fool.
> . . . A worthy fool! Motley's the only wear.
>
> (2.7.12–17, 34)

Jaques desires this role for himself, that is, the right to 'moralise' – or philosophise – rather than play the active masculine roles of his culture (it was he who criticised the hunting of deer). He uses Celia's word, 'liberty', here denoting freedom from conventional roles:

> I must have liberty
> Withal, as large a charter as the wind,
> To blow on whom I please: for so fools have.
> And they that are most gallèd with my folly,
> They most must laugh . . .
> Invest me in my motley; give me leave
> To speak my mind, and I will through and through
> Cleanse the foul body of th'infected world,
> If they will patiently receive my medicine.
>
> (2.7.47–61)

This is more of a fantasy than a real possibility for Jaques, for none of his moralising – even the famous 'All the world's a stage' speech (2.7.139–66) – has any effect on the play's plot. That is, he is actually already in the same category as Shakespeare's clowns, a watcher and commentator. He leaves the play at the end, unmarried, not included in any familial or political group. The fact, however, that his mordant observational mind has produced the play's most memorable speech brings him closer to the clown's role than he realises.[4] In drawing the analogy between the theatre where this very event is taking place and the 'seven stages' of human life, he is making the same sort of claim for the importance of art as Touchstone is in talking about the 'feigning' of poetry. It is likely that Shakespeare wrote this play for one of the first productions in the Globe, whose proud motto was 'Totus mundus agit histrionem' – all the world acts roles. Certainly, in Rosalind's extraordinarily active 'feigning' of the roles of woman, boy, and boy-woman, the audience has seen the truth of this.

A musical interlude: songs in the plays

Much Ado has one song, 'Sigh no more, ladies', performed by a character specially brought on to sing it (2.3). Its theme is 'Men were deceivers ever . . . the fraud of men' – a nicely ironic counterpoint to the easy belief of the male characters of the play that women are by nature deceptive. In modern productions this song is often reprised as the big chorus piece for the final dance – usually, however, without any sense of its irony.

In *As You Like It* there are, by contrast, five songs: two sung by Amiens, one of the exiled lords – 'Under the greenwood tree' (2.5) and 'Blow, blow thou winter wind' (2.7); the lords' triumphant hunting chorus in 4.2; the two boy pages' Elizabethan pop-song, 'It was a lover and his lass'; and a wedding song, introduced by the quasi-magical (or masque) figure of Hymen, 'Wedding is great Juno's crown' (5.4). As 'there's no clock in the forest' (3.3.254), music-making is a natural way of passing the time (there are no songs in Act 1), and commenting, to some degree, on the events of the day. Hence Amiens' two songs are musical versions of the exiled Duke's opening speech in 2.1 (the first satirised as idealistic nonsense by Jaques), and the ambivalences of the all-male 'horns' song. 'It was a lover and his lass' (for which we have the original music by Thomas Morley) and the wedding song fulfil the generic conventions of pastoral – sung by characters who otherwise only appear in small roles (if at all),[5] they are *pièces d'occasion* creating a mood of celebration of love appropriate to the play's optimistic ending: 'And therefore take the present time . . . for love is crowned with the prime'; ''Tis Hymen peoples every town. High wedlock then be honoured.' As Benedick might have sung – if he could sing – 'The world must be peopled!'

Twelfth Night

Twelfth Night, similarly, is full of songs, but they are all sung by one character, Feste the clown. Scholars point out that the role was probably written for Robert Armin, the company's new clown and a fine singer; this very fact makes his character more complex and integral to the play's themes than we have seen with earlier clowns. His professional role in the community requires him to provide music as well as jokes and banter. So, of the revelling Sir Toby and Sir Andrew he asks, 'Would you have a love-song, or a song of good life?' (2.3); he then performs a song with music by Morley, 'O mistress mine, where are you roaming?', with its melancholy reminder to the ageing knights that 'Youth's a stuff will not endure.' Feste's second song (2.4), also specifically requested – this time by Orsino: 'that piece of song, / That old and antique song we heard last night' – suits the self-indulgent Petrarchanism of Orsino, with its furniture of 'sad cypress' and 'black coffin' and claims of being 'slain by a fair cruel maid'. The actor playing Feste can choose how far he satirises Orsino's narcissism in his performance, but no amount of satire is likely to break the mood of the dialogue between Orsino and the disguised Viola, as they pursue their own emotional involvement with a coded discussion of 'constancy' in love. There are many other snatches of popular songs in the play, mostly about love (just like today's pop music), then finally Feste's epilogue takes the play out with his folk-like song 'When that I was and a little tiny boy'. This unsentimental piece provides a bridge for the audience back to the real world that they know, with 'knaves and thieves', unhappy marriages, and dismal London weather: 'And the rain it raineth every day.'

The play in fact begins with music, Orsino's often-quoted 'If music be the food of love, play on.' It establishes him immediately – as does everything else he says in this first scene – as consciously playing the role of the courtly lover, luxuriating in his own poetic performance, positively revelling in his lady-love's unattainability (he and Olivia don't actually meet face to face until the play's last scene). How much more enjoyable it is to use the 'suffering' of love for complete inactivity:

> Away before me to sweet beds of flowers:
> Love-thoughts lie rich when canopied with bowers.
>
> (1.1.40–1)

The entry of Viola, half-drowned, bereft of her beloved brother, in the next scene, operates as a powerful critique of this self-indulgence. The common practice of reversing the order of these two opening scenes to give Viola greater prominence as the protagonist is an interesting reflection of feminist-inflected thinking in the modern theatre, but the opening of the play as published, focusing on the enervated Duke of Illyria, can be just as thematically effective.

The eloquent heroine

Viola decides, at the end of her opening scene, to conceal her sex and disguise herself as her own twin brother, whom she believes drowned. Her decision to cross-dress is more emotional than practical (unlike Rosalind's); it is an act of memorialisation that carries with it the typical strain of melancholy to be found in this comedy. Moreover, Viola's story takes place *within* the class-bound society that the 'liberty' of Arden eschews (at least temporarily). As a page-boy, she loves the Duke, and is in turn pursued by a titled lady. Unlike Rosalind, who stage-manages everything but her father's court-in-exile in the forest, Viola is extremely constrained in her behaviour and her public speech. So, uniquely, she turns to the audience, and becomes a figure very like the clown, who has the freedom to speak across the edge of the stage to the 'real world' of the audience.

We can see this dynamic operating by contrasting two of Viola's most famous speeches, one in the *locus* of romance, one in the *platea* of the commentating clown. In Act 1 scene 5, her first interview with Olivia as Orsino's messenger, when asked by the intrigued Countess what 'he' would do if he were in love, Viola as Cesario replies:

> Make me a willow cabin at your gate,
> And call upon my soul within the house;
> Write loyal cantons of contemnèd love,
> And sing them loud even in the dead of night;
> Hallow your name to the reverberate hills,
> And make the babbling gossip of the air
> Cry out 'Olivia!' O, you should not rest
> Between the elements of air and earth
> But you should pity me.   (1.5.223–31)

Viola is here utilising the standard trope of poetic admiration from a distance, but by voicing female passion in a male convention, she reinvents it from within. This is astonishingly eloquent, passionate in a way that, clearly, Olivia has never heard before. The poetry is stunning: blank verse at its most expressive, with striking but simple imagery, supported by alliteration, assonance, and the rhythms of natural speech. Olivia is overwhelmed by this eloquent utterance, hailed into the experience of real desire – no wonder she responds 'You might do much!' So the high-born lady pursues the 'page-boy' throughout the play until such time as Sebastian turns up and re-establishes the normative heterosexuality (and class-structure) of romantic comedy. In this play Shakespeare is further pursuing an interest in the fluidity of gender and the unpredictability of desire that only months earlier he had explored in *As You Like It*. Olivia is not the first or the last character in *Twelfth Night* to fall in love with an unsuitable person.

In the course of indecorously signalling her interest in 'Cesario', she sends her disapproving steward Malvolio after him to give him a love-token, a ring. Viola refuses it and Malvolio peevishly throws it on the ground before exiting and leaving the stage to Viola, who can now safely address the audience in her 'true' persona, in a remarkable soliloquy:

> I left no ring with her: what means this lady?
> Fortune forbid my outside have not charmed her!
> . . . How will this fadge? My master loves her dearly,
> And I, poor monster, fond as much on him
> As she (mistaken) seems to dote on me.
> What will become of this? As I am man,
> My state is desperate for my master's love;
> As I am woman – now alas the day! –
> What thriftless sighs shall poor Olivia breathe?
> O time, thou must untangle this, not I;
> It is too hard a knot for me t'untie.   (2.2.14–39)

This very natural, conversational blank verse speech is not so much a self-communing as a chat to the sympathetic audience, who, after all, are the only people who share the secret of her identity, apart from the wrecked ship's captain. It's hardly 'poetical' (as Viola has said of her earlier prepared speeches on Orsino's behalf); it's full of questions, exclamations, broken-off thoughts. The odd bits of rhyme sound like a futile attempt to summarise a complicated situation. She reminds the audience of her femininity, and of the disparity between her 'outside' and her real self – such that she is a kind of 'poor monster', something unnatural, literally an outsider. Yet to stay thus disguised is her choice; in claiming that only 'time' can resolve the complicated issues, she is finally, clown-like, drawing the audience's attention to the pleasurable time that they are having watching this play.

At the very centre-point of the play Viola has another soliloquy that can be dynamically addressed to the audience. At the beginning of 3.1 two wanderers meet – Feste and Viola/Cesario. They exchange punning banter, about wit and words, and about the relation between professional and personal identity. Feste remarks, as he exits, 'Who you are, and what you would are out of my welkin – I might say "element", but the word is over-worn.' This cues Viola to turn to the audience to point out the similarity between these two characters in the play – the clown and the heroine:

> This fellow is wise enough to play the fool,
> And to do that well craves a kind of wit;
> He must observe their mood on whom he jests,
> The quality of persons, and the time . . .
>
> (3.1.50–4)

This, of course, is exactly what Viola in her chosen role as Cesario must do – live by her wit. In her doubleness – to be seen as much in her frequent word-play and riddling as in her deliberate gender ambiguity – Viola constantly shifts in the audience's perception between the pathos-inducing heroine of romance (who 'never told her love') and the self-aware, self-delighting performer/clown who, like Rosalind, is at the centre of her own play.

What, then, of the witty banter between unacknowledged lovers that we have come to expect in romantic comedies? Viola has only three scenes with Orsino – she has more with Olivia. Orsino is no Benedick; his typical utterance is highly 'poetical' (1.5.160) and self-obsessed. (Audiences might well wonder why Viola loves him – but one of the play's major themes is the suddenness and unexpectedness of love, or rather, desire – Cupid's fatal arrow.) Viola responds to this with her typical riddling,[6] here full of pathos:

My father had a daughter loved a man
As it might be perhaps, were I a woman,
I should your lordship.
ORSINO And what's her history?
VIOLA A blank, my lord. She never told her love,
But let concealment like a worm i'th' bud
Feed on her damask cheek . . .
ORSINO But died thy sister of her love, my boy?
VIOLA I am all the daughters of my father's house,
And all the brothers, too – and yet I know not.

(2.4.103–17)

In Viola's scenes with Olivia there is some word-play, but it has a curious air of desperation rather than delight – the engine of heterosexual flirtation is just not working. Instead we hear an almost incomprehensible exchange on outer appearance versus inner reality, concluding with the word 'fool' that reminds us that the scene began with Viola's riddling conversation with Feste:

OLIVIA Stay!
I prithee tell me what thou think'st of me.
VIOLA That you do think you are not what you are.
OLIVIA If I think so, I think the same of you.
VIOLA Then think you right: I am not what I am.
OLIVIA I would you were as I would have you be.
VIOLA Would it be better, madam, than I am?
I wish it might, for now I am your fool.

(3.1.122–9)

Viola's final short soliloquy takes the audience back to what is arguably the deepest emotional connection in the play – her love for her lost brother. When at the end of 3.4's farcical fight with Sir Andrew she is rescued by Antonio (who thinks she is Sebastian), she is left briefly at the front of the stage, to communicate to the audience her confusion and her barely admitted hope, in a speech of poignant rhyme and evocative imagery:

He named Sebastian. I my brother know
Yet living in my glass; even such and so
In favour was my brother, and he went
Still in this fashion, colour, ornament,
For him I imitate. O if it prove,
Tempests are kind, and salt waves fresh in love.

(3.4.330–5)

When the twins do finally meet in the play's *anagnorisis* (revelation of truth), this vein of poetic utterance is shared in a beautiful duet of recognition. Sebastian leads it:

> Do I stand there? I never had a brother;
> Nor can there be that deity in my nature
> Of here and everywhere. I had a sister,
> Whom the blind waves and surges have devoured.
> Of charity, what kin are you to me?
> What countryman? What name? What parentage?
> . . . Were you a woman – as the rest goes even –
> I should my tears let fall upon your cheek,
> And say 'Thrice welcome, drownèd Viola!'
>
> (5.1.210–15, 223–5)

Here Viola is called by her true name for the first time in the play. She no longer has a need either to make riddling jokes, or to reveal her thoughts to the audience: like the twins of *The Comedy of Errors* she has found her other half and is content. In fact, she speaks very little after this point in the final act: her last speech is the prosaic information that her 'maid's garments' are with the sea-captain, who has been detained by Olivia's steward – which allows the play to turn to dealing with that unresolved issue, the Malvolio story.

Puritans, revellers, and clowns

Critics categorise *Twelfth Night* as a romantic comedy because of its focus on the giddiness of love and the fluidity of gender, and the multiple marriages of its ending. But the play has an equally important second plot, that of the humiliation of Malvolio, the servant who is tricked into believing he can rise above his station. Elizabethan concern with class is at the centre of this plot: Malvolio's opponents are the drunken aristocratic parasites in Olivia's household, Sir Toby Belch and Sir Andrew Aguecheek, and Olivia's 'waiting-gentlewoman' Maria, the effective alternative head of the servant hierarchy. Maria is willing to be a class traitor because she is in a relationship with Sir Toby, and she gets her reward for siding with him when he marries her at the end of the play.

The revellers are introduced in the play's third scene – that is, they have equal dramaturgic importance with the Orsino plot and the Viola plot, which were introduced in Act 1 scenes 1 and 2. Their appearance creates a lively 'kitchen' world of the carnivalesque, the amoral realm of fleshly pleasure (roistering, 'capering', eating, drinking – and belching – and a bit of uncomplicated sex). 'I am sure care's an enemy to life', asserts Sir Toby in his opening speech. Malvolio, labelled by Maria a 'kind of Puritan', prefers repression and obsessive order to this thoughtless indulgence. This opposition (signalled by the word Puritan) would have been particularly resonant to the play's first audiences, for the Puritan movement was gaining increasing power among city merchants (who preferred sobriety and hard work in their apprentices rather than afternoons wasted at the theatre), and among religious leaders. It was to come to a head in the Civil War between the Puritan-identified parliament party and the High Anglican royalists that would have such a traumatic effect on England in the first half of the seventeenth century. All that was still in the future in the last years of Elizabeth's reign, but the particular opposition of Puritan (or Low Church) religious ideology to old practices (identified as Catholic) such as folk-festivals and church decorations, and to theatrical performances, was already making itself felt. Malvolio – whose name means 'ill-will' – is traditionally costumed in the severe black garb of the Puritan, which makes his climactic appearance before Olivia in yellow stockings, cross-gartered, all the more humiliatingly funny.

How he comes to this embarrassing self-exposure is neatly slotted between the events of the Viola plot, putting her romance in sharp contrast with something more like social realism (albeit an exaggerated, carnivalesque version). The 'kitchen scene', 2.3, which includes the clown Feste and his melancholy love song 'O mistress mine', is a performance of uninhibited 'caterwauling' drunken behaviour. Malvolio's interruption and complaint, if puritanical, is also justified:

> My masters, are you mad? Or what are you? Have you no wit, manners, nor honesty, but to gabble like tinkers at this time of night? Do ye make an alehouse of my lady's house, that ye squeak out your coziers' catches without any mitigation or remorse of voice? Is there no respect of place, persons, nor time in you?
> SIR TOBY We did keep time, sir, in our catches. Sneck up!   (2.3.75–80)

The roisterers' excessive, bullying revenge for having their fun stopped is to play on Malvolio's vanity, his personal weakness – Olivia has pointed out in 1.5 that he is 'sick of self-love . . . and taste[s] with a distempered appetite'. He will be fooled by this inflated idea of himself, and thereby turned unwittingly into a clown, a figure for laughter.

Malvolio's 'letter scene', Act 2 scene 5, is based on a very ancient comedy scenario: the pompous man, communing with himself about his greatness, encounters some physical object (puddle, banana-skin, dog-turd) that brings him down. The hidden onstage watchers who have set this up lead the real audience in malicious laughter and brazen commentary. Shakespeare's version is very sophisticated: it plays on the vanity of the 'lettered' among the servant-class (many in the play's first audience would still be functionally illiterate); the letter itself seduces Malvolio with its literary though 'fustian' (i.e. cliché-ridden) language. He is all too ready to see himself in the role of favoured lover – the real servant to the great lady become the Petrarchan poetic 'servant'. The actor playing Malvolio has a wonderful opportunity in this scene for physical comedy, 'practising behaviour to his own shadow', reading aloud and uttering unconscious obscenities ('her c's, her u's, and her t's, and thus makes she her great P's') and perhaps weird howls as he tries to make meaning out of 'M.O.A.I.'.[7] When he comes on in 3.4, following literally the absurd hints in the letter, in yellow stockings and cross-gartered, he has *visually* become a clown, in a type of motley: a circus-clown, rather than a jester, who does not have quick wit to defend himself. A basically pathetic figure, he gets unlooked-for laughs from his appearance: his lewd gestures and comments to Olivia, which he thinks are seductive, his inappropriate insistence on informing her of his physical problems – 'This does make some obstruction in the blood, this cross-gartering, but what of that?' His final reprise of the letter (3.4.58–73), in a triumphant soliloquy that can be played as a clown's monologue to the audience, is all about his fantasy of upper-class status, and nothing about his supposed love for Olivia. His grasp on the ambiguities of language is tenuous (he has no sense of humour, so can never read a double-meaning correctly): 'when she went away now, "Let this fellow be looked to" – "Fellow"! Not "Malvolio", nor after my degree, but "fellow"' (3.4.67–9).

The comedy here is basically cruel: although we laugh at his letter scene and his appearance in cross-gartered yellow stockings, we are laughing at the humiliation of someone less socially competent than ourselves. Shakespeare draws out the full implications of this perception: we are ultimately silenced by the heartless teasing of Malvolio by Feste and Sir Toby when he is confined to the dark house (4.2) – a scene that can have disturbing associations in modern productions. We are all too aware of the contemporary practice of torture by sensory deprivation; Malvolio's repeated cry, 'I am not mad' and his request for light and the means to write to the authorities have a chilling resonance. Even Sir Toby finally has a moment of sensitivity, 'I would we were well rid of this knavery' (4.2.53).

When Malvolio comes on at the end of the play, filthy and unkempt – and we hear that his letter has *not* been delivered – we have to acknowledge with Olivia that 'he hath been most notoriously abused'. The orderly household that he has tried, however oppressively, to maintain, has been turned topsy-turvy by the carnivalesque operations of unruly urges (his own included) – desire for non-stop parties, for sexual fulfilment, for class advancement. Between them Orsino and Olivia, as the leaders of the community, attempt to restore order: 'Pursue him, and entreat him to a peace.' But his uncompromising exit, with its grim promise to 'be revenged on the whole pack of you', is a dark note that disturbs the harmony of the 'golden time' that Orsino expects to follow the resolution of the play's romantic problems.

Chapter 6

Problematic plots and endings: clowning and comedy post-*Hamlet*

If Shakespeare's romantic comedy heroines have more in common with clowns than has been recognised – both being liminal characters that can comment on the story's images of order and hierarchy – then it may be helpful to think about the way clowns (and some heroines) function in a group of plays that can most simply be labelled 'post-comedy': *Measure for Measure, All's Well That Ends Well, The Winter's Tale, Cymbeline*, and *The Tempest*. There are, of course, clowns in other Shakespearean plays post-1600, notably the serpent-bringer in *Antony and Cleopatra* and the Porter in *Macbeth*, but their appearance, though crucial to both plot and theme, is in a self-contained scene. One example of this style of comic writing will suffice.

The opening of *Hamlet* 5.1 – the 'grave-diggers scene' – is one of the longest scenes written specifically for clowns in the Shakespearean canon. It follows immediately, in the Folio version, after Gertrude's lyrical account of Ophelia's drowning to her brother Laertes ('There is a willow grows askant a brook'). The two clowns (often, regrettably, reduced to one in modern productions) are onstage preparing Ophelia's grave. Their conversation begins as a pun-ridden vaudeville routine; the topic, suicide, the law, and class privilege. (Suicides were, under the law, forbidden burial in consecrated ground, but Ophelia is to be given a 'Christian burial' because of her status at court.)

> CLOWN It must be *se offendendo*, it cannot be else. For here lies the point: if I drown myself wittingly, it argues an act, and an act hath three branches – it is to act, to do, and to perform. Argal, she drowned herself wittingly.
>
> OTHER Nay, but hear you goodman delver –

> CLOWN Give me leave. Here lies the water – good. Here stands the man – good. If the man go to this water and drown himself, it is, will he, nill he, he goes – mark you that. But if the water come to him, and drown him, he drowns not himself. Argal, he that is not guilty of his own death shortens not his own life.
> OTHER But is this law?
> CLOWN Ay, marry, is't, crowner's quest law.
> OTHER Will you ha' the truth on't? If this had not been a gentlewoman, she should have been buried out o' Christian burial.
> CLOWN Why, there thou sayst – and the more pity that great folk should have countenance in this world to drown or hang themselves more than their even-Christen [fellow Christians].   (5.1.8–24)[1]

The clowns function here, as they do in the earlier plays, as speakers of the uncomfortable truths that can be spoken in a licensed situation – the theatre. The majority of Shakespeare's first audiences would recognise these truths with a wry smile: both secular and ecclesiastical 'law' are subject to the power of the class system. Enter Hamlet and Horatio, the epitome of the young intellectuals – for example, law students – that also were to be found in the audience. The punning exchange continues, but now the First Clown has a witty opponent, not just the second grave-digger's 'straight' man:

> HAMLET There's another. Why may not that be the skull of a lawyer? Where be his quiddities now, his quillets, his cases, his tenures, and his tricks? Why does he suffer this rude knave now to knock him about the sconce with a dirty shovel, and will not tell him of his action of battery? . . . I will speak to this fellow. Whose grave's this, sirrah?

There follows a sparky exchange of puns on 'lies', quite irrelevant to the dramatic situation, before the extraordinary third section of the scene. This part of the conversation provides an iconic image that has defined Hamlet for at least two centuries. The play's clown identifies the skull of a departed court jester, Yorick, and Hamlet addresses it:

> Alas poor Yorick! I knew him Horatio, a fellow of infinite jest, of most excellent fancy . . . Not one now, to mock your own grinning? – quite chop-fallen? Now get you to my lady's chamber, and tell her, let her paint an inch thick, to this favour she must come.   (5.1.156–64)

Although Feste may sing parodically of the lover's temptation to kill himself, and Cleopatra's clown may sardonically provide the means of the queen's suicide ('I wish you joy of the worm'), only Ophelia's grave-digger is the means of bringing the tragic hero face to face with a complex image of mortality: first in the form of the skull of the beloved jesting companion of his childhood, and then with the fresh corpse of his crazed, suicidal beloved. The image of the society that Hamlet once hoped to rule could hardly be bleaker: laughter, play, love, are all in a terrible state of entropy in a world that seems inherently corrupt.

Measure for Measure

Hamlet's grave-diggers are realists; no notion of the afterlife of the dead enters their earthy conversation. It might be argued that all Shakespeare's post-1600 clowns, starting with Jaques (who so obsessively identifies with Touchstone), are at base atheists: they see the world as it is, and tell the audience so. Only their social/theatrical role – as licensed sardonic commentators – protects them from being censured as agents of a creeping secularism in an England that was perhaps weary (and certainly wary) of talking about religion at all.

This perspective can help us understand the black comedy of *Measure for Measure*, a play written within a few years of *Hamlet*. Here Shakespeare offers another analysis of a society in a desperate state of corruption – this time, the contemporary city of Vienna, standing without much disguise for London itself. Vienna is ruled by a Duke who knows that he has lost control of the state: its good order is continually flouted by the citizens' fornication and drunkenness. He chooses to absent himself (abdicating his god-like authority) and puts in his place a deputy, Angelo (an apparent 'angel'), who has the reputation of icy self-control. But the Duke stays on, secretly, to watch (many modern productions even make use of surveillance cameras as part of the play's set-design).

This play, too, is fascinated by the fact of death in the midst of us, without any suggestion of an afterlife or Christian redemption. This attitude is strikingly encapsulated in Claudio's speech to his sister (Claudio is under sentence of execution for getting his fiancée pregnant):

> CLAUDIO Death is a fearful thing.
> ISABELLA And shamèd life a hateful.
> CLAUDIO Ay, but to die, and go we know not where,
> To lie in cold obstruction and to rot,
> This sensible warm motion to become
> A kneaded clod . . .
> The weariest and most loathèd worldly life
> That age, ache, penury, and imprisonment
> Can lay on nature, is a paradise
> To what we fear of death.
> . . . Sweet sister, let me live.   (3.1.116–33)

Isabella can save Claudio if she submits to Angelo's lust and allows him to take her virginity. She refuses this degradation ('More than our brother is our chastity'), and the situation is only resolved by the use of a 'bed-trick': Angelo sleeps with his former fiancée, Mariana, believing her, in the dark, to be Isabella. Angelo is then publicly humiliated and forced to marry Mariana, and the Duke proposes marriage to the intending nun Isabella at the end of the play. She does not answer – yet another example of the silencing of the heroine as the comedy concludes. *Measure for Measure* does conform to the comic model by ending with marriages, the resurrection of the apparently dead, and justice dispensed to all. But the marriages are forced, and there is little or no joy or sense of social regeneration at the play's end.

Where then is the comedy in this bleak fable? It resides in the substantial part of the play that depicts the behaviour of the low-life characters: they are given almost as much stage time as the serious high-status characters who carry the plot. Variously, Lucio, Froth, Pompey, Mistress Overdone, Elbow, Abhorson, and Barnardine appear in almost half of the play's scenes. They are denizens of pubs, brothels, the street, and the prison, and they are to a man and woman proud of their survival and pleasure-hunting skills. We might label them Falstaff's children. There is much in them, that is, for the audience to identify with – particularly as they provide the laughs that the grim story of Isabella, the Duke, and Angelo singularly eschews.

Lucio, in particular, is a major role. Described as a 'fantastic' in the Folio's cast-list – that is, 'an improvident young gallant'[2] – he is the spokesman for the pleasures of the physical life, and he has several striking interactions with the other-worldly Isabella. We meet him first in 1.2, and it is clear that he shares the clown's abilities in witty banter and punning: 'Behold, behold, where Madam Mitigation comes. I have purchased as many diseases under her roof as come to – '. Many jokes about the 'dolours' that venereal diseases cost follow. Mistress Overdone, however, brings news that their friend Claudio is arrested and 'within these three days his head to be chopped off . . . for getting Madame Julietta with child'. Lucio goes off immediately to try to help his friend. This leads to his first encounter with the novice nun Isabella, and a demonstration of his qualities as a gentleman despite his low-life habits:

> LUCIO I would not – though 'tis my familiar sin
> With maids to seem the lapwing, and to jest
> Tongue far from heart, play with all virgins so.
> I hold you as a thing enskied and sainted
> By your renouncement, an immortal spirit,
> And to be talked with in sincerity,
> As with a saint.
> ISABELLA You do blaspheme the good in mocking me.
> LUCIO Do not believe it.   (1.4.31–8)

Lucio speaks here in blank verse that poetically indicates his intellectual grasp of the issue and his sensitive and life-enhancing judgement of it:

> Fewness and truth, 'tis thus:
> Your brother and his lover have embraced;
> As those that feed grow full, as blossoming time
> That from the seedness the bare fallow brings
> To teeming foison, even so her plenteous womb
> Expresseth his full tilth and husbandry.
>
> (1.4.39–44)

Although Lucio never again rises to these poetic heights, his presence in the rest of the play often belies his 'fantastic' mask: he is present at Isabella's first interview with Angelo, and urges her on to greater eloquence as she begs for her brother's life in similarly poetic language. When he reappears in Act 3 scene 1 he returns to his man-of-the-world witty prose, but he speaks for the audience in making a satirical critique of the weaknesses of those in high places:

> LUCIO It was a mad fantastical trick of him to steal from the state and usurp the beggary he was never born to. Lord Angelo dukes it well in his absence: he puts transgression to't.
> DUKE [disguised as a friar] He does well in't.
> LUCIO A little more lenity to lechery would do no harm in him: something too crabbed that way, friar.
> DUKE It is too general a vice, and severity must cure it.
> LUCIO Yes, in good sooth, the vice is of a great kindred, it is well allied, but it is impossible to extirp it quite, friar, till eating and drinking be put down.   (3.2.82–92)

Unfortunately for Lucio, he gets carried away with his own wit, and next thing he is accusing the absent Duke of lechery and drunkenness and claiming to be his bosom companion. In the last act's return to 'normality' he is punished, as clowns sometimes are, for overstepping the boundaries of class respect. Forced to marry a prostitute whose child he has fathered, he exits with a last desperate joke: 'Marrying a punk, my lord, is pressing to death, whipping, and hanging!' The Duke's reply is, 'Slandering a prince deserves it' (5.1.514–16).

The play also features a cast of comic low-life citizens who are constantly at odds with the law as represented by constable Elbow, a near relative of *Much Ado*'s Dogberry, with the same facility for using the wrong word in unconsciously creative ways:

ELBOW First, and it like you, the house is a respected house; next,
this is a respected fellow; and his mistress is a respected woman.
POMPEY By this hand, sir, his wife is a more respected person than
any of us all.
ELBOW Varlet, thou liest! Thou liest, wicked varlet! The time is yet
to come that she was ever respected with man, woman, or child.

(2.1.141–6)

Pompey Bum, the tapster, is a comic masterpiece. He begins as a raconteur
in the best pub tradition who has no problems putting words together, as his
gloriously roundabout tale of Mistress Elbow and the stewed prunes demonstrates (2.1.81ff.). Obviously too good a clown (as the Folio speech-headings
label him) to be confined to Mistress Overdone's pub-cum-brothel, Pompey
gets a second role in the prison in which much of the action of the play takes
place. He appears there, briefly but significantly, at the play's fulcrum point,
Act 3 scene 1, and then enters into his full plot and thematic glory in 4.2 and
4.3: he becomes the deputy executioner. Like *Hamlet*'s grave-digger, Pompey's
jesting about the profession's 'mystery' is a way of bringing the stark reality of
death onto the stage, yet allowing the audience to laugh at it for the time being,
since death here is clearly absurd: supposedly under the control of men, it will
be defeated by the generic spirit of comedy. In 4.3 this perception is played out
in the absurdly comic scene in which Barnardine simply refuses to be executed.
Pompey exhibits inappropriate politeness: 'Master Barnardine, you must rise
and be hanged, Master Barnardine! . . . You must be so good, sir, to rise and
be put to death.' Barnardine replies with imperturbable, drunken finality, after
a considerable discussion which includes the Friar/Duke, 'Not a word. If you
have anything to say to me, come to my ward, for thence will I not today' – and
returns to his cell.

This scene offers a fantasy that all audiences can share: that we have control
over death, here represented by the figures of secular authority (the disguised
Duke), of religion (the Duke as friar), and of institutionalised murder (the pair
of bumbling executioners). In the optimistic spirit of comedy, Barnardine is
reprieved and freed by the Duke at the end of the play: his commitment to
going on living (and drinking) is as important as the marriages with which the
play ends. Perhaps more so, since those marriages all appear to be tainted by
their association with authority and the law, which the play's major plot-line
has strongly critiqued. Lucio must marry his whore (though he had previously
deserted her), and in a parallel resolution, Angelo must marry Mariana, whom
he had previously jilted. Claudio will marry Julietta – but their premarital
sex is spoken of by the Duke simply as a 'wrong' that must be 'restored' (in

contrast to Lucio's sense of their mutual response to natural drives). And Isabella, the play's tough and humourless heroine, may or may not accept the Duke's out-of-the-blue offer of marriage. The Duke – a restored but now questionable authority-figure – parrots the word 'love' in relation to both his offer and Angelo's marriage. The play seems to argue that the word is a romantic delusion, and that only sex makes the world go round.

All's Well That Ends Well

Another play from the early years of the seventeenth century, *All's Well* similarly problematises love and marriage, the staples of romantic comedy. It too is highly conscious of mortality, exemplified in age, illness, and war. Yet its heroine, Helena, is a more complex and active figure than the single-minded Isabella – she is something closer to Rosalind. She has quasi-magical powers, being the daughter of a famous doctor. But she is also a young woman, subject to the irrational force of sexual desire – and Bertram, the young man whom she loves, despises her as socially beneath him. The play's plot involves much travelling for the heroine: she comes into contact with a wide range of society and has to make unassisted decisions about what actions will best serve her drive towards self-fulfilment. She has a profession – healing – and a desire to be loved by a particularly unworthy callow young man. Altogether Helena is an interestingly modern figure, and the play is easily translatable into modern terms; the plot could make a good Hollywood romantic comedy.

The story to a large extent re-mobilises the themes of *Much Ado About Nothing*. It is driven by an overt conflict between men and women. The male culture is symbolised by soldiering (in modern terms it could be football): a world of drinking, male competition including teasing amounting to bullying, and an attitude to sexual relations that is all about trophy-collecting (pretty virgins, preferably). Marriage is approached reluctantly, and only if there is clear financial or social gain to be had. Feminine culture is symbolised by the work of healing, a mutually supportive female community, and an attitude to sexual relations that is dependent upon maintaining virginity until 'Mr Right' comes along and offers marriage – or Mr Good-enough, given the limitations of masculine culture.

Helena embodies many characteristics of both Beatrice and Hero, Bertram many of both Benedick and Claudio, in driving this plot of gender conflict. Their wit is not employed on each other – like Hero and Claudio, they barely speak to each other in the course of the play – but is evident in their scenes with Parolles, the effete man of 'words' (as his name indicates – *parole* is French for 'word') whose role is to channel popular thought: about sex and virginity (with Helena), and about soldiering and masculinity (with Bertram). Parolles is a gentleman wit, like Lucio or Jaques; but this very wittiness disbars him from true (active) masculinity. On the other hand, it gives him a direct line of connection to the audience, like the professional clown (in this play, Lavatch) whose role he often subsumes. Before we examine the difficult relationship of Helena and Bertram, then, we should look at what Parolles helps us to see about each of them. (It's worth remembering here that Shakespeare the playwright is also a 'man of words'.)

In exactly the same position as Beatrice and Benedick's first conversation in *Much Ado*, i.e. in the second half of Act 1 scene 1, Helena engages in witty banter with Parolles. The subject is virginity: we already know (having been privy to her soliloquy at lines 78–104) that she loves Bertram (who has said just one line to her before he exited: 'Be comfortable to my mother, your mistress, and make much of her.') Note the military metaphor with which she begins the discussion – the war of the sexes (no longer a '*merry* war' as in *Much Ado*) is still the norm in gender relations:

> HELENA Ay. You have some stain of soldier in you: let me ask you a
> question. Man is enemy to virginity; how may we barricado it against
> him?
> PAROLLES Keep him out.
> HELENA But he assails, and our virginity, though valiant, in the
> defence yet is weak. Unfold to us some warlike resistance.
> PAROLLES There is none. Man, setting down before you, will
> undermine you and blow you up.
> HELENA Bless our poor virginity from underminers and blowers-up!
> Is there no military policy how virgins might blow up men?
>
> (1.1.99–108)

At this point Parolles begins a virtuosic riff on the word 'virginity' and what it represents in 'the commonwealth of nature':

> Loss of virginity is rational increase, and there was never virgin got till
> virginity was first lost. That you were made of, is metal to make virgins.
> Virginity by being once lost may be ten times found; by being ever kept
> it is ever lost . . .
>
> Virginity breeds mites, much like a cheese; consumes itself to the very
> paring, and so dies with feeding his own stomach. Besides, virginity is
> peevish, proud, idle, made of self-love, which is the most inhibited sin in
> the canon. Keep it not; you cannot choose but lose by't. Out with't!
> Within ten year it will make itself two, which is a goodly increase, and
> the principal itself not much the worse. Away with't!   (1.1.112–28)

The audience cannot but notice that the topic is being signalled as central to the play to come. What, however, might well surprise them is Helena's next question: 'How might one do, sir, to lose it to her own liking?' This is no prude. Parolles' advice is to seize the moment of her youth and physical desirability, and not to languish after 'him that ne'er it likes. 'Tis a commodity will lose the gloss with lying; the longer kept, the less worth.' Helena's heartfelt response, however, shows that she is besotted with the contradictory Bertram:

> His humble ambition, proud humility,
> His jarring, concord, and his discord, dulcet,
> His faith, his sweet disaster . . .   (1.1.146–8)

Clown-like, Parolles moves between social groups. When we next see him, in 2.1, he is at the King of France's court, encouraging Bertram to 'steal away' to the wars in order to cultivate his homosocial bonds:[3]

> Use a more spacious ceremony to the noble lords; you have restrained yourself within the list of too cold an adieu. Be more expressive to them, for they wear themselves in the cap of the time, there do muster true gait; eat, speak, and move under the influence of the most received star, and though the devil lead the measure, such are to be followed.   (2.1.48–54)

It is clear from both scenes that the man of words understands social structures and processes. His emotional dependence on Bertram, however, is his Achilles' heel: it is signalled by his rare use of blank verse, with its ability to suggest subtext:

> To th' wars, my boy, to th' wars!
> He wears his honour in a box unseen,
> That hugs his kicky-wicky here at home,
> Spending his manly marrow in her arms,
> Which should sustain the bound and high curvet
> Of Mars's fiery steed. To other regions!
> France is a stable, we that dwell in't jades;
> Therefore to th' war!   (2.3.254–62)

Parolles is in love with 'manliness', and this speech also indicates his personal distaste for sexual activity involving women ('A young man married is a man that's marred', 2.3.275). It is this that drives him to boast of his own military exploits, and it leads to his downfall. The two Lords Dumaine constitute the brotherhood that Bertram wants to be part of, and their test of Bertram is to propose a trick on Parolles to demonstrate his cowardliness (3.6). Following the model of homosocial bonding, this scene ends with Bertram persuading one of the Lords Dumaine to go with him to look at the 'cold' girl, Diana, that he fancies: she will be, like the epicene Parolles, a commodity passed between them that seals their bond.

There follows a short scene (3.7) between Helena and the Widow that shows a different type of bonding – working together towards a positive outcome, that of forcing Bertram to accept the responsibilities of marriage, via the romance-narrative favourite, the bed-trick (as in *Measure for Measure*). This is in strong contrast to the scenes of Parolles' capture and subsequent humiliation that take up much of Act 4. Although such a teasing and public humiliation of the braggart soldier has occurred in earlier Shakespearean and other drama – in particular, with Falstaff in *1 Henry IV* and *The Merry Wives of Windsor*, a twenty-first-century audience is likely to be made very uncomfortable by the extensive use of disorientation and sensory deprivation techniques used here. The image of a blindfolded Parolles, spoken to in a language he cannot understand (it is nonsense), is reminiscent of modern military 'coercion' techniques. Memories of Abu Ghraib are hard to avoid, and a modern director might even choose to evoke them in these scenes: a forceful display of the ugly underbelly of military glory and its ideology of male comradeship. Bullying – whether of captured opponents or of those perceived to be effeminate members of their own side – is endemic in most armies. Nevertheless, the play conforms to the optimistic model of comedy in this as in the other plot-lines: Parolles is left alone to contemplate his humiliation, and he concludes the scene with a soliloquy that not only offers wisdom to the audience, it shows him accepting his true profession as a clown – and thus, the audience's friend and point of connection:

> Simply the thing I am
> Shall make me live. Who knows himself a braggart,
> Let him fear this; for it will come to pass
> That every braggart shall be found an ass.
> Rust, sword; cool, blushes, and, Parolles, live
> Safest in shame! Being fooled, by fool'ry thrive!
> There's place and means for every man alive.
>
> (4.3.280–6)

The next time we see Parolles (5.2) he is bantering with Lavatch, the Countess's jester; and Lafew (whom he had insulted when a soldier) magnanimously offers him a place, perhaps as the 'fool' he now acknowledges himself to be. His quick fluency with words – a professional qualification for a fool – is still on display in the play's last scene, and contributes to its clarification and dénouement. Parolles survives, finding himself a social role that is markedly neither masculine nor feminine: the gossip, the sharp-tongued observer, the clown. This type of role will have a long future in English drama, often combined with that of the fop – notably, at various points in *All's Well* we have heard of Parolles' knotted scarves, handkerchiefs and elegant Spanish accoutrements. Of course, as an acknowledged fool he is entitled to dress outlandishly ('Motley's the only wear', as Jaques says, longingly, in *As You Like It*).

For Helena, however, the journey is longer and harder, and perhaps ultimately unresolved although she ends up with a husband, and carrying his child. As the play's heroine, Helena is remarkable for her eloquence – and for the fact that it is largely directed to other women, or to the audience, in an impressive array of soliloquies. The number of lines she speaks to her beloved, Bertram, is just thirty in the whole play. *All's Well*, then, does not conform to the basic model of romantic comedy. What is Shakespeare offering his audience? As Steven Mentz argues, it is a story that combines two recognised female archetypes from medieval narrative, the clever woman (actively outwitting authority) and the patient sufferer: 'The play gives dramatic form to the competition between two major early modern genres, the novella and romance, and their nearly opposite ideologies.'[4] Mentz calls these the 'Doctor She' and 'Idolater' plots: 'They function as mutual antidotes: when the novella-story seems too racy or disorderly, the moral solidity of romance rescues it, but when a purely passive heroine promises theatrical dullness, witty tricks return to the play' (66–7). This mixing of genres – and therefore of audience expectations – will become more common towards the end of Shakespeare's writing career, in what are now called the 'late romances' (which I discuss below). Arguably, then, the playwright is deliberately moving away from the comedy formula that served him well up to 1600, creating ever more radical challenges to his audience, and perhaps pursuing the hope of a commercial hit with a new formula.

Helena's role is an astonishing one for a boy actor, though it is on a par, in terms of complexity, with other female roles written at about this time: Cleopatra, Lady Macbeth. We are, presumably, looking at a role written for a very talented boy of perhaps fifteen or sixteen years – no child. Helena is eloquence personified, and her intellectual achievements and personal charisma are recognised by everyone but Bertram. This includes the audience, who are taken into her confidence in 1.1, as she comments to herself and us on the subtext of the scene we've just seen, that of the Countess's farewell to her son:

> My imagination
> Carries no favour in't but Bertram's.
> I am undone! There is no living, none,
> If Bertram be away. 'Twere all one
> That I should love a bright particular star
> And think to wed it, he is so above me.
>
> (1.1.70–5)

Like Phebe in *As You Like It*, she is prey to desire, besotted by Bertram's physical beauty:

> 'Twas pretty, though a plague,
> To see him every hour; to sit and draw
> His archèd brows, his hawking eye, his curls,
> In our heart's table – heart too capable
> Of every line and trick of his sweet favour.
> But now he's gone, and my idolatrous fancy
> Must sanctify his relics.   (1.1.80–6)

Her fast switch from this evocation of maidenly romantic longing to bawdy banter with Parolles (discussed above) demonstrates Shakespeare's exploration of new ground in characterisation. But there is more to come, at the end of this same scene: a soliloquy that offers some general wisdom to the audience, and at the same time indicates that this woman intends to pursue her desires:

> Our remedies oft in ourselves do lie,
> Which we ascribe to heaven. The fated sky
> Gives us free scope; only doth backward pull
> Our slow designs when we ourselves are dull.
> . . . Impossible be strange attempts to those
> That weigh their pains in sense, and do suppose
> What hath been cannot be. Who ever strove
> To show her merit that did miss her love?
> The king's disease – my project may deceive me,
> But my intents are fixed, and will not leave me.
>
> (1.1.187–200)

This challenge to act, and to achieve, will be assisted throughout the play by a group of other women working in solidarity with Helena. Here the model is that of the racy novella rather than the genteel romance (in the latter the heroine, if she is active, tends to be alone and subject to terrifying trials). The play's first line is spoken by a woman, the Countess: this is the only play in the Shakespearean canon in which a female voice is heard first (if we except, as we may, *Macbeth*'s witches). She is a figure of social, moral, and emotional authority; the more so in that all the male characters in the play, including the sick King of France, are variously lacking in maturity or strength. In a long straight-talking scene between Helena and the Countess (1.3), this dynamic of support is established: the Countess insists on seeing her as a spiritual daughter, not just daughter-in-law. The Countess, unlike her son, is unworried by Helena's lowly class status, and more than willing to see her prove herself as a professional healer – implicitly, to show herself worthy of Bertram's and other men's respect: 'be sure of this, / What I can help thee to thou shalt not miss' (1.3.227–8).

Helena has two scenes (2.1 and 2.3) with the King of France before the play's final scene. The first demonstrates her professional confidence – she has been announced as 'Doctor She' by Lafew (2.1.75), and she talks more than the King does, convincing him to try her remedy. The second begins with the King leading her onstage, and demonstrating his cure by dancing a 'coranto' with Helena, then sitting her beside him. These are high marks of respect indeed in a court structured on male hierarchy, but Helena, as she chooses a husband under the King's newly vigorous eye, is no longer talkative. Her professional skills (which women were not expected to have) ironically enough have restored the masculine status quo. The scene's dynamic switches to a conflict between Bertram and the King – which the King, of course, wins. But the marriage he insists on, we learn at the end of the scene, will be in name only: 'Although before the solemn priest I have sworn, I will not bed her', swears Bertram to his bosom-pal Parolles (2.3.246–7). This failure even to attempt kindness to his wife is heart-breakingly emphasised in the tiny scene of parting between Bertram and Helena (2.5): she asks for a kiss, he rudely ignores the request and tells her to hurry off. Helena, here modelled on the suffering woman of romance, responds, 'I shall not break your bidding, good my lord.' These are the last words they exchange until the play's conclusion.

Helena's mid-play soliloquy (3.2.91–121) does not appeal directly to the audience: it is inward-looking and self-blaming; its only outward appeal is to 'thee', the idolised but absent Bertram. It is a lonely moment for Helena, as she determines to set off, like the heroines of old romances, on a pilgrimage – in effect, to become a homeless wanderer. This she conveys by letter (actually an accomplished sonnet) to the Countess, who is also shown to be emotionally isolated:

> Which of them both
> Is dearest to me I have no skill in sense
> To make distinction . . .
> My heart is heavy, and mine age is weak;
> Grief would have tears, and sorrow bids me speak.
>
> (3.4.38–42)

At this central point of the play, the lowest point for the two women who had begun it so confidently, we are introduced to a new group of energetic no-nonsense women. Note the original stage direction: 'A tucket afar off. Enter an old Widow of Florence, her daughter [Diana], Violanta, and Mariana, with other citizens.' Noise, cheerfulness, a clear change of place, and lively chat among this group of mutually supportive women: what a relief it is to the audience to see, as Helena enters 'dressed as a pilgrim', that her wanderings have led her here. She, the Widow, and her daughter Diana agree that the bed-trick (whereby Helena will take Diana's place as Bertram makes love to her) is an appropriate means of bringing about sexual justice, and the play proceeds to its dénouement via a ring-exchange plot (as in *The Merchant of Venice*, the sexual punning on 'rings' is clear).

Helena has let the rumour spread that she has died of grief (4.4.11). Any actor playing Bertram will feel that there is a scene missing here: that in which he is informed of Helena's death, and reacts to it. The mourning for Helena is instead verbalised by the old people, Lafew and the Countess, in 4.5, towards the end of which the substitution used to humble Claudio in *Much Ado* is proposed – here, apparently, in good faith, as Lafew presumably does not know that Helena is alive. The fact that the scene also features Lavatch, the Countess's fool, in word-play with Lafew, suggests to the audience (who know the true state of affairs) that the mode of comedy will triumph and all will end well.

The play's ending remains, however, uncomfortable, and a challenge to directors and actors who want to explore its analysis of gender relations. Helena's death is somewhat perfunctorily mourned as all the characters gather in Roussillon: Bertram declares that since he has heard of his loss he has 'loved' her, and the King, Lafew, and the Countess proceed to organise his marriage with Lafew's unseen daughter Maudlin. It is only the display of rings exchanged in the bed-trick that disrupts this neat ending – that, and the noisy eloquence of Diana, here standing in for Helena as Helena once slipped into Diana's place in bed with Bertram. Diana, in the last 180 lines of the play, has all the expla-nations and exclamations of innocence that we might have expected Helena to utter. She concludes her expostulations with word-play:

> Dead though she be, she feels her young one kick.
> So there's my riddle: one that's dead is quick.
>
> (5.3.292–3)

'And now behold the meaning', she says, as (anticipating Paulina of *The Winter's Tale*) she draws all eyes to Helena and the Widow entering. Helena is noticeably pregnant, the embodiment of the answer to Bertram's contemptuous riddle: '"When from my finger you can get this ring, / And are by me with child, etc." This is done.' The two women, Helena and Diana, assisted by Diana's mother the Widow (representing also that other present but silent widow, the Countess), have, if not the last word, certainly the strongest presence in the play's final moments. Helena and Bertram enter into their married life on the basis of conditionals:

BERTRAM If she, my liege, can make me know this clearly,
I'll love her dearly, ever, ever dearly.
HELENA If it appear not plain, and prove untrue,
Deadly divorce step between me and you!   (5.3.305–8)

And although the King, as befits his status, makes the last summarising speech, in which he claims 'All yet seems well', it is interesting that after a 'Flourish of trumpets' he then reveals himself as simply the chief player, begging for the audience's applause in the Epilogue. The fable is just a fable; 'all's well' is the hopeful conclusion of the genre of comedy, which rarely coincides with the realities of the world, where 'seeming' is perhaps the best one can hope for. Helena and Bertram, in their final relationship, are much closer to the disturbing model first presented by Hero and Claudio; the shared wit that we saw uniting Beatrice and Benedick now operates only in the separate camps of women and men.

The late romances

The term 'romance', not used in the First Folio's table of contents, was applied to a group of late Shakespearean plays by scholars in the nineteenth century – *Pericles*, *The Winter's Tale*, *Cymbeline*, and *The Tempest*.[5] This 'new' genre should not be confused with the form of medieval tale known as a romance (French *roman*), which Steven Mentz uses to help us think about the heroine of *All's Well*; the Shakespearean 'late romances' are a law unto themselves, particularly in their rambling plot-lines (though *The Tempest* is an exception in this regard). Many plot elements and character types are, however, shared with those of the earlier comedies. There is a 'happy' ending, though as we have seen that generic joy is often shadowed by doubt about the strength of the marriages thus concluded, in the face of real-world pressures and conventions – and particularly the habitual gender behaviours that we have seen operating throughout the play. There is also, invariably, the presence of death: not realistically portrayed on stage (as in the tragedies and histories), but as news reported of one of the major characters (most often female). A process involving loss, grief, and remorse is built into the play's story-arc, enabling an ending that reveals the lost to be found, the apparently dead brought back to life. Emotionally, this moment in the play's last scene – which often involves rediscovering lost family members, a brother, a daughter, a wife – can be more engaging than the happy union of lovers, the dancing and feasting that traditionally takes a play out on an upbeat note. Throughout his career as a writer of comedy, Shakespeare celebrates family reunion: the Dromio twins, Rosalind and her father, Viola and Sebastian, and finally Hermione and Perdita.

Helena's return at the end of *All's Well*, visibly pregnant, to a world that thinks her dead, foreshadows to some degree the 'miraculous' ending of *The Winter's Tale*. Pregnancy is of course the most obvious symbol of a world with the hope of renewal, but the abused Hermione, whom we had seen pregnant in Acts 1–3 of *The Winter's Tale*, at the end of the play meets her grown-up daughter Perdita whom she had thought destroyed as a new-born by her husband Leontes. The emotional complexity of this scene is extraordinary, and very challenging to all involved in performing it. Add to it that Hermione appears in this final scene as a statue brought to life before her now repentant husband, and the word miraculous barely does it justice. Shakespeare here is daring all, in order to claim the regenerative powers of art itself; and although we undoubtedly have a happy ending, 'comedy' has seemed too light a term to apply to the solemnity of these final moments on stage. The same can be said of the endings of *Cymbeline* and *The Tempest*.

Nevertheless, Shakespeare was still in important ways developing the genre of comedy in these three plays, and threaded through all of them are familiar figures – most notably, various types of clowns and the standard situations in which they tend to get involved.

The Winter's Tale

The Winter's Tale is boldly constructed. It takes almost three acts to set up its apparently tragic plot: Leontes believes that his wife Hermione has been unfaithful with his best friend Polixenes; he imprisons her though she is pregnant. He is told that she has died in bringing forth the child, and their young son dies of grief. But the female baby has been abandoned by old Antigonus on a distant shore, where he hopes that she will be found and cared for. At this point, exactly halfway through the play, comedy enters – Antigonus makes an almost farcical exit to his death: 'Exit pursued by a bear' (3.3.57).[6] It is probably the most radical shift of mood in all of Shakespeare.

The Old Shepherd and his son (the latter simply labelled 'Clown') provide a classic two-person comedy duo. Each has the gift of prolixity; in ways that suit the separate characters of youth and age, each tells, in tumbling, energetic prose, material of great moment that connects the first half of the play (tragic) with the second (comic). The Old Shepherd begins with his complaint on the sexual shenanigans of the young, such as the audience might hear by any pub fireside:

> I would there were no age between ten and three-and-twenty, or that
> youth would sleep out the rest; for there is nothing in the between but
> getting wenches with child, wronging the ancientry, stealing, fighting
> [etc.].   (3.3.58–61)

Aptly, he finds the bundle containing the baby Perdita and her worldly goods.
The tone is still comic, and appeals knowingly to the audience:

> What have we here? Mercy on's, a bairn! A very pretty bairn. A boy or a
> child, I wonder? A pretty one, a very pretty one – sure, some scape;
> though I am not bookish, yet I can read waiting-gentlewoman in the
> scape. This has been some stair-work, some trunk-work, some
> behind-door work; they were warmer that got this than the poor thing is
> here.   (3.3.66–72)

Taking up the child, his further cogitations are interrupted by the excited arrival
of his son, the Clown, who has 'seen two such sights by sea and by land!' and
cannot decide which to tell of first. The consequence is a comically confused
narrative which the audience, who have prior knowledge, can unpack:

> O, the most piteous cry of the poor souls! Sometimes to see 'em, and not
> to see 'em; now the ship boring the moon with her mainmast, and anon
> swallowed with yeast and froth, as you'd thrust a cork into a hogs-head.
> And then for the land-service, to see how the bear tore out his
> shoulder-bone, how he cried to me for help and said his name was
> Antigonus, a nobleman. But to make an end of the ship, to see how the
> sea flap-dragoned it; but first, how the poor souls roared, and the sea
> mocked them; and how the poor gentleman roared, and the bear
> mocked him, both roaring louder than the sea or weather . . . the men
> are not yet cold under water, nor the bear half dined on the gentleman –
> he's at it now.   (3.3.82–96)

The Old Shepherd, who embodies folk wisdom (compare Corin in *As You Like
It*), pithily draws our attention to the play's shift in mood and genre: 'Thou
met'st with things dying, I with things new-born' (3.3.101). The baby's 'fairy
gold' is an added bonus that reassures us that this fairy-tale turn to the story
will not involve hardship or deprivation. Nor will it lack love: the Old Shepherd
and his son have good hearts and good wills, and the scene's final line drives
home the change of mood: ''Tis a lucky day, boy, and we'll do good deeds
on't.'

The play then takes a sixteen-year break, personified by Time, the Chorus –
a metatheatrical moment in which the mythical figure draws attention to the
audience's choice of 'spending time' with this romantic tale of lost children.[7]

He introduces the information that Perdita is happily 'grown in grace', and that Polixenes has a son, Florizel, of similar age. Obviously they will form the happy royal couple that will renew Leontes' poisoned realm. We meet them in the midst of a sheep-shearing festival. Here Shakespeare re-mobilises the pastoral genre that he had transformed in *As You Like It* some eight years earlier. It is done with great nonchalance, an almost over-the-top deployment of pastoral tropes: songs, dances of satyrs and of shepherds and shepherdesses, witty courtship dialogues between Perdita and the disguised Florizel. And a 'rogue', a sophisticated conman who goes by the name of Autolycus, who introduces himself to the audience with a song and the confidential information that he is 'a snapper-up of unconsidered trifles' (4.3.25). Autolycus sings and steals and tricks his way through the rest of the play. He has no vital plot function: he is, rather, an embodiment of the spirit of anarchy that Shakespeare's cleverest earlier jesters were not quite brave enough to admit to, being place-servers all as a matter of personal preservation. His literary antecedents are in fact the 'cony-catchers' of Elizabethan popular literature, denizens of the city who live by their wits and are subject to no master. This is the clown as modern survivor: salesman, entertainer, confidence trickster. The play's original audiences would have recognised him and roared with laughter – for once, they are in the secret of the conman's tricks: it's an empowering, feel-good perspective.

It's also somewhat revolutionary. There is an aesthetic question as 4.3 begins: how will this embodiment of the modern, real world, by choice a masterless man, combine with the 'high' fairy-tale romance that depends upon our respect for royal hierarchies? For all the subversive delight that Autolycus provides in 4.3 and 4.4, as the naïve pastoral community is pickpocketed and variously cheated, he is ultimately drawn into the service of the young royal lovers. The disguised prince, Florizel, changes clothes with the always-in-disguise conman. This is a type of magical transformation: we may subconsciously register that Florizel is all the better a potential king because he knows how to use the anarchic energies that Autolycus embodies. As Autolycus reflects, speaking to the audience:

> I understand the business, I hear it. To have an open ear, a quick eye, and
> a nimble hand is necessary for a cutpurse; a good nose is requisite also,
> to smell out work for th'other senses . . . The Prince himself is about a
> piece of iniquity, stealing away from his father with his clog at his heels.
> If I thought it were a piece of honesty to acquaint the King withal, I
> would not do't; I hold it the more knavery to conceal it; and therein am I
> constant to my profession.   (4.4.642–52)

Autolycus demonstrates his protean genius, using his new clothes (those of a courtier) to bully and con the Old Shepherd and his son (who *still* doesn't recognise Autolycus, though he has now encountered him in three guises). Ultimately, the genre of fairy-tale wins over that of urban comedy, and the last we see of him is in conversation with these two rustic clowns ('those I have done good to against my will', 5.2.105), who have been raised to gentry status by a grateful king. Their transformation gives them authority, and even to the Clown some worldly wisdom:

> CLOWN [to Autolycus] Give me thy hand. I will swear to the Prince
> thou art as honest a true fellow as any is in Bohemia.
> SHEPHERD You may say it, but not swear it.
> CLOWN Not swear it, now I am a gentleman? Let boors and franklins
> say it, I'll swear it.
> SHEPHERD How if it be false, son?
> CLOWN If it be ne'er so false, a true gentleman may swear it in the
> behalf of his friend; and [to Autolycus] I'll swear to the Prince thou
> art a tall fellow of thy hands and that thou wilt not be drunk; but I
> know thou art no tall fellow of thy hands and that thou wilt be
> drunk; but I'll swear it, and I would thou wouldst be a tall fellow of
> thy hands.   (5.2.134–45)

In its smaller way, this transformation of the country clown into a courtier and gentleman is as extraordinary as the play's 'miraculous' ending, that celebration of the power of art to return the dead to life.

Cymbeline

There is no named clown in *Cymbeline*, a sprawling narrative set in a fiction-alised Roman Britain and focusing on the adventures of the last of Shakespeare's cross-dressed heroines, the princess Innogen, who has married a commoner. But perhaps there is a clown – one who has lost the ability to charm the audience with his comic shtick. There are some very funny scenes involving the loutish Cloten, son of Innogen's wicked stepmother. His profound sense of self-importance makes him something of a Bottom without the sexual naivety. 'A pox on't', he complains in his first scene (2.1), 'I had rather not be so noble as I am' – because all he wants to do is fight. He has also been put up to wooing Innogen by his crafty mother: when she roundly rejects him he sulks and vows revenge for her comment that her husband Posthumus' 'meanest garment' is dearer to her. Like a not very bright schoolboy bully he tells the audience that his revenge will be taken in a suit belonging to Posthumus:

> Even there, thou villain Posthumus, will I kill thee. I would these garments were come. She said upon a time – the bitterness of it I now belch from my heart – that she held the very garment of Posthumus in more respect than my noble and natural person, together with the adornment of my qualities. With that suit upon my back will I ravish her; first kill him, and in her eyes; there shall she see my valour, which will then be a torment to her contempt. He on the ground, my speech of insultment ended on his dead body, and when my lust hath dined – which, as I say, to vex her I will execute in the clothes that she so praised – to the court I'll knock her back, foot her home again. She hath despised me rejoicingly, and I'll be merry in my revenge.   (3.5.128–39)

This energetic – and potentially laughter-inducing – prose is the last remnant of Cloten's clown-like eloquence. He also speaks a lot of rather dull blank verse, in his capacity as member of the royal family; but in his final appearance, the scene in which he is killed by the king's lost son Guiderius, we have the unusual comic phenomenon of blank verse written to sound deliberately 'low' – that is, Cloten speaks in a blustering, inelegant way that allows the audience to laugh heartily at the scene of his comeuppance (and death):

> CLOTEN Thou villain base,
> Know'st me not by my clothes?
> GUIDERIUS ... Thou art some fool;
> I am loath to beat thee.
> CLOTEN Thou injurious thief,
> Hear but my name, and tremble.
> GUIDERIUS What's thy name?
> CLOTEN Cloten, thou villain.
> GUIDERIUS Cloten, thou double villain, be thy name,
> I cannot tremble at it.   (4.2.80–90)

The true king's son has identified Cloten as an overweening 'fool' (as his plebeian name suggests); his demise cannot trouble us because he has brought it on himself. 'Cloten's clotpoll' is thrown into the river like that of the ogre in a fairy-tale.

His decapitated body, placed beside the drugged Innogen, serves as a macabre stage property to convince the heroine on waking that her husband has been murdered. The play returns to a world of emotional trauma and heartbreak, a territory it occupies till its very last moments, when the dénouement once again offers a scene of the return of those thought lost or dead, and reconciliation of the married lovers. Responses of relieved and incredulous laughter often accompany the one-a-minute revelations of the last scene, and it is perhaps a mistake to try to play it all in high seriousness: just as in *The Comedy of Errors*, the audience is reassured that the threat of death and the disintegration of family has miraculously disappeared, and all is right with the world.

The Tempest: postscript

What was once farcical violence (as in so much of *The Comedy of Errors*) returns in Shakespeare's late plays as true violence, with real consequences in the real world. It would require magic for this not to happen – and perhaps an island, cut off from the world. In *The Tempest* the real, political world's citizens find themselves brought to an island ruled by a magician; and the play's plot, in righting old wrongs and bringing about a blessed marriage, still conforms – just – to the model of comedy. It has two clowns: Trinculo, the King of Naples' jester, and Stefano his drunken butler; and briefly, in 2.2 Caliban, the 'savage' native of the island, plays a comic role as he tastes liquor for the first time. But Caliban is unique, a far more complex figure than the servants of the King: he is as likely to break into lyrical poetic verse as to curse his master. The drunken scenes for Trinculo and Stefano offer good opportunities for classic physical clowning, but they can get tedious if not performed by extraordinarily inventive clowns. Like Caliban (and like Sebastian and Antonio), the two servants want to seize the opportunity apparently offered them to upset the laws of social hierarchy, and become rulers (and gain possession of the one young woman on the island). But this threat is nugatory, since the audience knows that all is under the control of Prospero, who can create illusions and command the winds. The artist-magician has announced himself at the beginning of the play, and comedy's chance events are never allowed to surprise us. The clowns exit ignominiously from the play; they have no double-edged words of wisdom and commentary to offer at its close. That, of course, is left to Prospero, the artist-magician, who reminds us of the ambivalent power of the artist whose operations we have witnessed for the foregoing two hours:

> release me from my bands
> With the help of your good hands.
> Gentle breath of yours my sails
> Must fill, or else my project fails,
> Which was to please.

Was it? we might ask, or was Shakespeare's 'project' more mysterious, less congenial, in this late, uniquely structured play?

Chapter 7

The afterlives of Shakespeare's comedies

At the end of *Love's Labour's Lost* Biron is given a task by his lady-love Rosaline, to spend a twelvemonth visiting 'the speechless sick':

> your task shall be
> With all the fierce endeavour of your wit
> To enforce the painèd impotent to smile.

The clever man, who has talked his way out of many difficult situations, is taken aback:

> To move wild laughter in the throat of death?
> It cannot be, it is impossible.
> Mirth cannot move a soul in agony.
>
> (5.2.834–9)

We might guess that the role of Biron is Shakespeare's fantasy version of himself as a young man obsessed by language and its relation to the real world of power, love, sex, class, and community.[1] What is the role of wit? Can it have any power to do good? Biron would like to think so, but it is a big call. The ladies, fully aware of the real world and its demands – suffering, death, and the 'world-without-end bargain' of marriage (5.2.777) – have chosen not to make this play's 'sport' a 'comedy'. So the audience has had both a comedy and not a comedy, both laughter and frustration. Perhaps, from this young writer early in his career, what is being signalled here is the possibility of a *new* version of comedy – more complex, emotional, unpredictable.

Not long after writing *Love's Labour's Lost* Shakespeare undertook a major experiment in expanding the parameters of comedy: *The Merchant of Venice*. The courtroom scene (4.1) in this play is an extreme case of the complexity and unpredictability that Shakespeare brought to this genre. Set in a court of law, with an authoritative figure presiding, it begins in grimness and desperation: Shylock is determined with 'lodged hate and a certain loathing' to have his pound of flesh from Antonio, who is there in the court opposite him. The Duke's efforts to call upon the ideal of mercy (just like Portia's a little later) are futile; they are met with Shylock's reminder that in the real world that they all inhabit (not the world of benign, mercy-filled comedy),

> You have among you many a purchased slave,
> Which, like your asses and your dogs and mules,
> You use in abject and in slavish parts
> Because you bought them.   (4.1.90–4)

The law makes human bodies expendable; what follows from this principle is the murder Shylock is proposing to enact on the body of Antonio. The climax of the scene is the tense sequence in which Shylock prepares to cut into Antonio's bare breast. A black comic style can be called upon here: a macabre performance of knife-sharpening, preparation of the scales, bowl, and napkin. In this case the audience is in the enjoyable realm now familiar in the Hollywood horror-flick genre. Equally, the moment can be underplayed, a calm, appalling, inexorable ritual. Portia's 'Tarry a little' at the last possible moment interrupts the planned (and law-approved) murder with a classic example of the 'improbable fiction' of comedy:[2] if the audience doesn't necessarily laugh at this point (that will depend upon the build-up of the scene), there will certainly be a sigh of relief. The clever young woman has brought about what no male seemed able to do: she has outwitted patriarchal law, whether it be that of the writers of the Old Testament or that embodied in the Duke of Venice. One of the basic rules of comedy – the triumph of the resourceful young woman – has been reasserted, and 'all shall be well' (*Dream* 3.2.463). Except that Shylock is dismissed from the stage with more of the humiliations and baiting that have brought about his desire for revenge on the 'Christians' in the first place. Shylock's position in the real world remains unresolved. The world, in short, is benign for some, a place of suffering and oppression for others. Shakespeare's mature comic style recognised and incorporated this; and what follows is that performances of the plays in different times and cultures can draw out different emphases, different moods, different meanings.

Comic fictions and historical reality

Anti-semitism has a long and appalling history in western Christian culture. Purges and pogroms against Jewish communities came to a head in the mass murders of millions of European Jews in the first half of the twentieth century; this reality radically shook the folk-tale-based tradition of Shylock as the bogey-man. But in fact the reading of Shylock as a tragic figure predates the mid-twentieth century's horrors by some 200 years. Interest in the figure of the 'outsider' in literature (Othello is an early example) was fuelled by the eighteenth-century Enlightenment project of sensibility – what we might call empathy, feeling for the sufferings of others. Shylock also appeals to this mind-set because he is the father of a daughter who deserts him. Images of the grieving father are a powerful antidote to those of the murderous money-lender. Although there was a minor tradition of continuing to play Shylock as an exaggerated comic villain (in a rewritten version of the play by George Granville, 1701), by the mid-eighteenth century actors were taking up the role as an addition to their tragic repertoires,[3] and their performances were enthusiastically reviewed. Jane Austen noted of Edmund Kean's younger and more complex Shylock, which she saw in the great actor's first London season, 'in his scene with Tubal there was exquisite acting.'[4] Reviewers in the twentieth century rarely comment on this scene (3.1); but in the nineteenth century its pathos was often underpinned by a near-silent, mimed scene, in which Shylock returned to his house at the beginning of 2.8, to find it empty, his daughter having fled.

This traditional sympathetic interpolation is almost always made in films of the play. Michael Radford's 2004 film, starring Al Pacino as Shylock, insists on its realism and historical accuracy in the depiction of sixteenth-century Venice, as did Jonathan Miller's BBC Time-Life production (1980, directed by Jack Gold). Film gives a greater opportunity than most stage productions can to show the Jewish community at home in the ghetto – including religious observances – and interacting with the Christians in business on the Rialto. Many directors of both stage and film versions will take an early opportunity (as Radford does) to show a silent encounter between Shylock and Antonio – the latter spitting contemptuously at Shylock.

These films offer an educative experience for modern viewers, showing them the long history of anti-semitism that led to the Holocaust. There is no question that this is both a noble and a necessary use of Shakespeare's play. What is routinely denied in pursuit of this aim is the play's comic aspect. Lancelot Gobbo rarely survives, or does so only as a shadowy messenger of the plot. Portia and Nerissa in the Belmont scenes seem often to be more sad and oppressed by their situation than seizing the opportunities for bawdy jokes offered them by the text. The dark undertones of the Shylock story shadow Michael Radford's Belmont at the end of his film, so much so that the viewer has fears for the happiness of the marriage about to be consummated between Portia and Bassanio – her sense of betrayal seems to come between them, as does the continuing focus on the sad and lonely Antonio (who is not told, in this film, that his fortune has been recovered).

Performance history, social history

In the Induction to *The Taming of the Shrew* a befuddled Christopher Sly asks, 'Is not a comonty [comedy] A Christmas gambol, or a tumbling trick?' 'No, my good lord', replies Bartholomew, 'It is a kind of history.' By this he means, primarily, an entertaining story; but the two words are etymologically the same, and we are justified in working with an assumption that every 'story' told by a community to itself tells us something about the 'history' of that society: its own view of what it thinks about gender relations, sexuality, power, money, and other things that make the world go round.

The Shrew is a particularly interesting case in point. We know that it was developed by Shakespeare from a standard tale of wife-taming that exists in dozens of forms in the medieval period and the earlier sixteenth century. We can also infer that something about this story led him to put a 'frame' around it, to invite us to see it as the fantasy of a coarse, drunken tinker – whose character is partly transmogrified into the figure of aggressive and successful masculinity, Petruchio. The play's first revival after the English Revolution was James Lacy's adaptation, *Sauny the Scot*; this was a vehicle for the author's comic talents in the role of Sauny (Grumio), his 'crass jokes . . . constantly upstag[ing] the taming narrative', which itself was rewritten to suit Restoration tastes (for example, including a bedroom scene).[5]

David Garrick, the great eighteenth-century actor and entrepreneur, had a mission to bring back Shakespeare's texts (rather than their Restoration alterations) to the English stage. He put together from Shakespeare's play, without the Sly frame or most of the Bianca story, a two-act farce called *Catharine and Petruchio*. Elizabeth Schafer comments, 'the overall effect of the adaptation was to produce a simple, farcical battle of the sexes, which proclaims the duties wives have to submit and makes *The Taming of the Shrew* seem a masterpiece of ambiguity and complexity by comparison' (11). It also shifted the focus in the play's last moments to Petruchio, the triumphant husband, who speaks the last lines of Katherina's original speech and then indicates that henceforward he will be a kindly husband. Hugely successful, it held the stage (displacing Shakespeare's original) for a hundred years.

With the growth of feminism in the late nineteenth century, gradually the focus moved away from the hyper-masculine Petruchio and onto the more problematic figure of Katherina. Shakespeare's complete play was revived authoritatively in an 1887 production by the American Augustin Daly, starring Ada Rehan, a tall, imperious woman who brought emotional complexity and upper-class manners to her relationship with Petruchio (for contemporary reviews, see Schafer 15). Women's agitation for the vote (it was not gained in England till 1928) brought new nuances to the play, and also vocal protests against Katherina's last speech from women in the audience in early twentieth-century productions (Schafer 25). Second-wave feminism, in the last quarter of the twentieth century, brought the most radical re-readings of *The Shrew*. Katherina's performance of her final speech became the most eagerly antic-ipated moment of the play: would it be 'ironic, sincere, angry, exhibitionist, lobotomised, in love, masochistic, feminist, indulgent, threatening, or does she just have her eyes on the cash?' (Schafer 34). The actress's choice here, of course, finally reflects back on her relationship with Petruchio (and with her family) in the course of the play's events. How cruel, teasing, tender, pedagogical, ther-apeutic, have Petruchio's actions been? And has it been possible for Katherina to negotiate a viable personal autonomy in the face of this treatment? As with Shylock, some moments in the play would seem now to be unplayable in the 'traditional' way. Petruchio's relentless starving and humiliation of the newly married Katherina in Act 4 is perhaps the major example.[6]

Films of *The Taming of the Shrew*, of which there have been many, have tended to opt for a simple, conservative reading, with an emphasis on farcical action, very little by way of actual brutality, and strong sexual chemistry between the two protagonists. The Katherinas all finally submit, but never without a fight – and, in fact, Katherina's shrewishness is usually reconfigured into a restless and impatient energy which manifests itself in furniture-throwing and the teasing of boring goody-goody Bianca. A certain amount of subversion of Kate's last speech is usually permitted: from Mary Pickford's wink at the camera in the 1929 film (with Douglas Fairbanks Snr) to Elizabeth Taylor's disappearance into the crowd as Petruchio (Richard Burton) celebrates his 'victory'. Franco Zeffirelli's 1967 film, like Jonathan Miller's version for the BBC Time-Life series (1980), sets the story in a 'realistic' sixteenth or seventeenth-century environment. For this to work and convince the audience that what they are watching is social history, the Sly frame disappears. What can't be made to disappear, however, is the extra-diegetic (offstage) associations that the films' stars carry with them. Thus, audiences of Zeffirelli's film 'knew' that they were watching some version of the Burton/Taylor romance (and Burton's notorious drinking). John Cleese played a strong Petruchio in Miller's 'historical' version, but nothing will stop the audience from seeing him as a Python or Basil Fawlty and mapping that onto the figure of Petruchio, whatever Miller may have intended by this casting.

The fact that film is a stable text that can be re-viewed indefinitely, and can thus offer historical insights into the life and times of its makers, is cleverly negotiated in the film of *Kiss Me, Kate*, the phenomenally successful 1948 musical by Sam and Bella Spewack with music by Cole Porter. In its turn, this musical was based on the famously fiery stage partnership of American actors Lynne Fontane and Alfred Lunt. The film, made in 1953 (director George Sidney) with the original Broadway stars Kathryn Grayson and Howard Keel, uses as its 'frame' two once-married actors who have been brought together for a musical production of *The Taming of the Shrew*. The film's first scenes (or Induction) take place at a rehearsal of the new songs in the apartment of Cole Porter. Throughout this smart and exhilarating film, the audience is never allowed to forget the artificiality of its situation, and if it still panders to the Hollywood romantic ending, along the way Grayson/Lilli/Katherina has had the opportunity to sing the brilliantly witty post-war feminist anthem 'I Hate Men'. Porter's music and the Spewacks' lines together provide the Katherina-figure with more agency than might previously have ever been imagined.

The play's ultimately conservative fable, combined with the sexual charisma of its two stars, is the perfect model for Hollywood romantic comedy. Arguably, the Katherine Hepburn/Spencer Tracy movies of the 1940s and 1950s, for example *Woman of the Year* (George Stevens, 1942), are distant adaptations of *The Shrew*, and their model is still powerful, if not quite so blatantly conservative, in modern Hollywood. The high-school comedy *10 Things I Hate About You* (Gil Junger, 1999) has a plot consciously based on Shakespeare's play, in which the clever but spoilt Julia Stiles is wooed by the unconventional Australian student, Heath Ledger. Once again, Petruchio wins in the charisma stakes: the highlight of his wooing (even though it is for a bet) is a full-scale performance of 'Can't take my eyes off you' complete with brass band, in the school's sports arena. Kat's capitulation, by contrast, is her weepy public reading of her own not very good poem. *The Taming of the Shrew* remains an extremely potent model for a reinforcement of conventional gender relations, made palatable by sexy stars and rollicking physical farce.

Romantic comedy and its heroines

As might be expected, feminism in the broadest sense has had its most marked influence on productions of the three great romantic comedies, with their central female roles. What is surprising is that these three plays – *Much Ado about Nothing*, *As You Like It*, and *Twelfth Night* – virtually disappeared from the repertoire between the publication of the First Folio in 1623 and the Shakespeare revival of the 1740s. Productions of the tragedies and the major histories continued unabated throughout the Restoration period, though most were comprehensively rewritten to suit Restoration tastes. But the genre of comedy was largely represented in the Restoration and early eighteenth century by new plays. Restoration comedy was set in the city (usually contemporary London); it satirised recognisable male figures at the court of Charles II; it was overtly raunchy, its main plot line being the adventures of a libertine. Such plays would have at least one clever and witty young woman, who usually resisted the rake's advances until he promised marriage in the play's last scene. These young women, however, are given very little stage time compared with the depictions of the masculine world of libertine gentlemen and fops, their servants and the tradesmen whom they all despise. The Restoration comedy that is probably most admired today, Congreve's *The Way of the World* (1700), was in its day not very successful. The play's most memorable scene is the 'proviso scene' between the sparring lovers Mirabell and Millamant. Reminiscent, in all their encounters, of Beatrice and Benedick, in this scene they go beyond them to establish, with coruscating wit, a pre-nuptial agreement that includes both personal autonomy and mutual support. A new ideal of masculinity, under the aegis of a monarchy that was now the embodiment of domestic virtue (Queen Anne and the Hanover kings who followed her), was represented on stage in such 'sentimental comedies' as Richard Steele's *The Conscious Lovers* (1722). Actresses – who had only been appearing on the English stage since 1660 – were by now equal stars with the men, and the way was opened for the revival of Shakespearean romantic comedy.

George C. D. Odell, the first modern historian of Shakespeare on the stage, remarks that Drury Lane theatre 'unexpectedly' in 1740–1 put on *As You Like It, Twelfth Night,* and *The Merchant of Venice,* 'for the first time practically in a hundred years, all, I believe, inspired by the ambition of Macklin, who acted Touchstone (though not at first), Malvolio and Shylock'. The following year *All's Well* and *The Comedy of Errors* were added to the Drury Lane repertoire. 'The ladies of the Shakespeare Club no doubt were instrumental, to some extent, in urging the manager to this so desired end. All these influences, however, were probably but scattered manifestations of the rising tide of romanticism, which was sweeping through literature and life.'[7] What Odell calls 'romanticism' we might more accurately see as the growth in the valuing of 'sensibility' that I commented on earlier: a feminisation of public expression in the arts, which made space for the skills and charisma of a new breed of professional actresses.

Much Ado had had a partial revival in 1737 as *The Universal Passion,* by James Miller. It was hybridised with a Molière play, but from Act 3 onwards the play returns to Shakespeare, with additional dialogue, and songs for the Beatrice-figure Liberia, who was played by the rising star Kitty Clive. The full return to Shakespearean text began in 1741 at Drury Lane with a production of *As You Like It*: with 'Caelia by Mrs. Clive, Rosalind by Mrs. Pritchard. The Songs new Set by Mr. Arne. With Entertainments of DANCING' at the end of Acts 1, 3, and 4, performed by French solo dancers.[8] The two female stars of Drury Lane, Clive and Pritchard, were now drawcards along with James Quin's Jaques. Demonstrating their accomplishments, the ladies were expected to sing (which neither Rosalind nor Celia does in the original): Arne wrote a setting of 'When Daisies Pied' (from *Love's Labour's Lost*) to fill the gap – sung first by Clive as Celia; in years to come, Rosalinds would often appropriate it. Odell writes of 'a succession of great Rosalinds in the eighteenth century – Mrs. Pritchard, Mrs. Woffington, Mrs. Barry, Mrs. Yates. Measure for Measure was revived at times to give these same fair ladies an opportunity to appear as Isabella' (Odell I, 339). He later points out that '*As You Like It* was more frequently acted from 1776 to 1817 than any other Shakespearian play at Drury Lane . . . [But] at Covent Garden, where there was less talent on the distaff-side' (i.e. actresses), the play was rarely performed (Odell II, 20).

David Garrick's influence on bringing more Shakespearean comedies back to the stage, from 1747 when he took over management of Drury Lane theatre, was immense – though he was not above a clever filleting of a play perceived as old-fashioned, or just simply too long, such as *The Taming of the Shrew*. Garrick encouraged and employed a succession of star actresses, as noted above; and his own genius in comedy (as well as tragedy) meant that Benedick in *Much Ado* became a popular part. Benedick, as I argued in chapter 5, is not a heroic or even romantic lover; he has strong affinities with the clown. The quicksilver Garrick's success in the role is further evidence of a change in popular notions of masculinity.

The printed 'acting edition' of Shakespeare, published by John Bell in 1773, 'regulated from the prompt-books, by permission of the managers', demonstrates that although the comedies were often cut (frequently for reasons of decency), and songs were automatically added, the texts performed by the middle of the century were reasonably true to the originals. Occasionally a few more lines were added to the end of the play to make a more satisfactory romantic ending: the example given of the Duke's proposal to Isabella in *Measure for Measure* certainly makes that event seem less peremptory and more public-spirited:

> Shade not, sweet saint, those graces with a veil,
> Nor in a nunnery hide thee; say thou'rt mine;
> Thy Duke, thy Friar, tempts thee from thy vows.
> Let thy clear spirit shine in Publick life;
> No cloister'd sister, but thy Prince's wife.
>
> (quoted in Odell II, 25)

No doubt eighteenth-century Isabellas, offered an ascent to the aristocracy (as was so often the case with popular actresses), accepted graciously.

The succession of great comic actresses continued unabated: Elizabeth Younge, Frances Abington, Dorothy Jordan, at the end of the eighteenth century; and in the nineteenth century Fanny Kemble, Helen Faucit, Ellen Tree, and the visiting American Ada Rehan, whose feisty Katherina and Rosalind were a sensation. The nineteenth-century list concludes famously with Ellen Terry, who made Beatrice and Portia very much her own roles, adding to their wit a tenderness that Victorian ideas of femininity demanded. *Measure for Measure* and *All's Well* once again virtually disappeared from view. Both, of course, depend for their resolution upon a 'bed-trick' orchestrated by the heroine; it is no wonder that Victorians were reluctant to encounter these plays and their unorthodox heroines. It should be noted here that two other favourite roles for Victorian actresses and their audiences were Hermione in *The Winter's Tale* and Imogen (Innogen) in *Cymbeline* – both ideal models of suffering femininity. Most of the clowning and 'low' comedy in these plays was cut in production, and the focus was firmly on the heroine's brave endurance.

Filming the comedies

With a twentieth-century model of more active (and talkative) femininity generally accepted, productions of the romantic comedies became common-place occurrences. But it took a while for the movie industry to catch up, enthralled as they still were by the hero-focused tragedies and histories. Apart from the succession of *Shrew* films, discussed above, the only notable films of the comedies in the first half of the twentieth century were Reinhardt's *A Midsummer Night's Dream* (1936), most notable for its Mechanicals and Puck (Mickey Rooney), and an *As You Like It* (Paul Czinner, 1936) starring the young Laurence Olivier as Orlando and the German actress Elisabeth Bergner as Rosalind – the latter struggling somewhat with the language in an intermittently amusing film.

There are now many films of stage productions adapted for television, which can offer thought-provoking records of directorial concepts and actors' performances. But the translation of stage plays into another artistic medium, that of film, using all its potential to tell a predominantly visual version of the story, is still relatively unexplored (there are more film versions of Jane Austen's novels than of the Shakespearean comedies to which they are so clearly related). The late twentieth-century films I discuss below offer different examples of how cinema can make its own art out of Shakespearean comedy.

Generally, there are five models of Shakespeare films:

(1) The 'historical', which purports to represent the real world that the play is set in, e.g. Radford's *Merchant* or Zeffirelli's *Shrew*, both discussed above. The datedness of the latter made in 1967 (with fashionable contemporary hair-styles, make-up, music), demonstrably undermines claims that it is possible to 'faithfully' represent the sixteenth-century world.

(2) The Shakespearean text, but set in a different historical period which thereby imposes certain interpretative emphases: Branagh's *Much Ado*, discussed below, Nunn's *Twelfth Night*, set in fin-de-siècle Victorian Cornwall; Hoffman's *Midsummer Night's Dream*, set in fin-de-siècle Italy; Branagh's *As You Like It*, set in nineteenth-century Japan.

(3) The 'period hybrid', in which much of the Shakespearean text is substituted with other more popular texts, often musical: Branagh's *Love's Labour's Lost*, discussed below, and the Spewacks' *Kiss Me, Kate*. Both have 'frames' providing a more recent historical perspective.

(4) The modern-dress setting using Shakespeare's text, which patently sets out to demonstrate the modern 'relevance' of Shakespeare, translating it usually into a big-city setting: Edzard's *As You Like It*, discussed below; Luhrmann's *Romeo + Juliet*.

(5) The modern 'translation', in which plot and characters are kept, but the dialogue is rewritten (and radically shortened) in modern colloquial English (*10 Things I Hate About You*, discussed above; *She's the Man*, a teen high-school version of *Twelfth Night*) – the purpose here being to clarify for a contemporary audience gender and social issues that are identifiable in the Shakespearean story and still relevant in the modern setting. The BBC Shakespeare Retold series of four plays (2006) included two comedies in its line-up: *Much Ado* and *A Midsummer Night's Dream*.

Some examples follow.

Kenneth Branagh's film of *Much Ado About Nothing* (1993), a 'period' production,[9] starred himself as Benedick and his then wife Emma Thompson as Beatrice. Branagh chose a vaguely Regency style of costume – not historically realistic but romantic and sexy: men in tight breeches, women in uncorseted low cleavage and flouncy skirts. The setting is a travelogue-style Tuscan villa – a middle-class person's holiday fantasy. Branagh claims in his introduction to the published script that he wanted 'utterly real' characters, and realistic performances in a 'realistic background' – but he also admits that the 'imaginary world' his designers created 'was distant enough to allow the language to work without the clash of period anachronisms and for a certain *fairy tale* quality to emerge . . . Tuscany, a magical landscape . . . that seems untouched by much of modern life' (italics added).[10] So the 'realistic' emotional story takes place in a world that we can only inhabit in our fantasies, a Hollywood film world.

This fine line between realism and romance is signalled in the confident opening sequence of the film. In a paradisal landscape, Beatrice is a little separate from the others – she has literally a better view of the world (up a tree), and she is reading the song from Act 2 about the battle of the sexes, 'Sigh no more ladies . . . Men were deceivers ever'. It is her voice, not Shakespeare's or some anonymous singer's, that speaks. She is less 'innocent' than everyone else here: the opening of the film gives Beatrice a moral and intellectual authority that she never loses. The men arrive in a phalanx on their horses, over the title – the shot is a conscious homage to *The Magnificent Seven* (1960), a classic Western about a 'band of brothers'. Whereas Beatrice is first seen separate from her group, Benedick is very much part of his. The men, stripping naked to bathe, look as though they are entering innocently into the paradisal world; there is childish horseplay and glee. But they get back into their uniforms, not into mufti, and march in military formation into Leonato's courtyard to confront the ladies (who have also been shown bathing excitedly and dressing up). The overhead shot that finishes this opening sequence shows the meeting – or will it be confrontation? – of the masculine and feminine worlds.

The acting, from a transatlantic all-star cast, is often thrilling. Thompson and Branagh's performances as Beatrice and Benedick are both funny and passionate. The 'Kill Claudio!' scene (4.1) concentrates simply on these fine actors delivering Shakespeare's words, with some artful use of the chapel's large cross in the background to give symbolic underlining. To render the 'fairy-tale' unlikeliness of the clowns being the guardians of the law, Branagh turns to Hollywood tradition, utilising the physical comedy of the 1920s and 1930s: Michael Keaton's Dogberry and Ben Elton's Verges are modelled on duos such as Abbott and Costello. Keaton's deliberately inarticulate performance substitutes for Dogberry's verbal clowning a violent slapstick. Branagh commented that he wanted to create a sense of 'danger' for the audience in having an almost-certifiable Dogberry, the town bully: 'the audience feels uncertain about whether the plot will ever truly resolve itself' (Branagh xiii), since Dogberry is so madly self-absorbed, like a petty gangster or the cop who is pursuing him. Thus to the escapism of a Tuscan landscape Branagh adds edgy urban black comedy.

The alienation of twentieth-century urban life is the theme of Christine Edzard's *As You Like It* (1992). If, as Jaques famously says, 'All the world's a stage', then that stage is now the global city. This film takes 'exile' in Arden to be the waste lands of the city's homeless, who live on the edge of the luxurious offices of big business and finance. This is a thought-provoking rendition of the play, though the romance of Rosalind and Orlando comes off a poor second to the film's stern social critique. Kenneth Branagh's 2007 film of the play takes a very different tack, returning to the successful model of his *Much Ado*, but this time setting the escape-world in a fantasy of nineteenth-century Japan – albeit populated largely by western characters.

Musical comedies

Adding music to a Shakespearean comedy was a popular practice in the seventeenth century: the heavily re-written *Tempest* (1667 and 1674) added a spicy touch of Restoration comedy by having Miranda (the girl who had never seen a handsome young man) echoed with Hippolito (a boy who lives on the other side of the island, who had never seen a pretty young girl; he eventually meets and falls in love with Miranda's sister Dorinda. Only the Restoration audience could have accepted this absurdity). These additions by Dryden, Davenant, and Shadwell were accompanied by a substantial anthology of music by different hands. Thomas Arne's settings of Ariel's songs in *The Tempest* (1740), notably 'Where the bee sucks', are so charming that they are still occasionally used today; the plot was returned to its normal Shakespearean cast by 1838.

Similarly, *A Midsummer Night's Dream* was rendered 'operatic' in 1692, when Purcell's musical talents went to the creating of self-contained masques that ended each act of the play and reflected obliquely on the events of the plot. (The masques did not involve the familiar characters of the play.) The operatic treatment of the play continued: following Garrick's brief musical *The Fairies* (1755), in 1816 Frederick Reynolds did a full-scale version of the play, with interpolated songs and music by Henry Bishop and others, and much dancing and spectacle. The play was given its most familiar musical accompaniment in Mendelssohn's charming music for a popular production by the enterprising theatre manager and actress/singer Eliza Vestris (1840). This gave prominence to the fairy world, a peculiar obsession of the Victorians; its image of fairies in white frocks with gauze wings is still commonplace in the popular imagination.[11] Benjamin Britten's 1961 opera, a fully sung version of the play, makes the fairies much more sinister, Oberon in particular, who was sung by the then unfamiliar counter-tenor voice (the role had usually been played by a woman in the nineteenth century, notably by Mme Vestris, in tights). But Britten also has fun with the play's farcical aspects, writing a very funny fight scene for the lovers, and a hilarious parody of early nineteenth-century grand opera (specifically *Lucia di Lammermoor*) for the Mechanicals' play.

The more farcical comedies have fared better in musical adaptation than a play such as *Twelfth Night*, despite the latter's original text being more obviously musical. Feste's songs in *Twelfth Night* were usually cut in the eighteenth and nineteenth centuries (apart from 'When that I was and a little tiny boy'), and songs added for Olivia instead. Frederick Reynolds had as great a success with his *Comedy of Errors* (1819) as with *A Midsummer Night's Dream*, possibly because the shortness of the play and simplicity of the plot left room for what the early nineteenth-century audience apparently wanted: 'Songs, Duets, Glees, and Choruses' – the arranger of all this music being once again Henry Bishop. Song texts were from other poems and plays by Shakespeare, indiscriminately adopted. Additional scenes were written by Reynolds to allow for these musical extravaganzas, for example a snow-clad hunting scene in Act 3 in which 'When icicles hang by the wall' (from *Love's Labour's Lost*) was sung in full chorus.[12] Reynolds did then go on to attempt his musical magic on *Twelfth Night* (1820), but it was not as great a success (Odell II, 136). And as Odell remarks, the law of diminishing returns set in conclusively with his 'operatisations' of *The Tempest* (1821) and *Two Gentlemen of Verona* (1821).

But 'the longest-lived of Bishop and Reynolds's re-workings of Shakespeare into the operatic mould was The Merry Wives of Windsor' (1824) (Odell II, 140). Like *The Comedy of Errors*, it is a tightly plotted play that can easily be shorn of minor scenes in order to accommodate more music. Fenton and Anne Page, obvious roles for tenor and soprano, were matched with a comic mezzo-soprano role for Mistress Page. At least two later operatic versions of *The Merry Wives of Windsor* were composed – by Nicolai (1849) and Verdi (1893). Verdi's *Falstaff* has been the most successful of these, neatly trimming the fat of the play and writing strongly characterised musical roles for all the main characters, in particular the baritone Falstaff, one of the great operatic roles. The opera ends with a headlong fugue to the words 'Tutto nel mondo è burla' – 'everything in the world's a joke'.

Perhaps unconsciously reiterating Reynolds' practice in popularising Shakespeare, Kenneth Branagh's 2000 film of *Love's Labour's Lost* is a musical version done in the style of the Astaire/Rogers films, mixing Shakespeare's dialogue (heavily cut) with the songs of the 1920s and 1930s. Naturally, Kern's song 'I won't dance' is given a major song-and-dance treatment, the sentiment moved from Shakespeare's Act 5 to the first meeting of the gentlemen and ladies. Branagh sets the play in the thirties, using commentary in black-and-white newsreel style to give a wider political context – the build-up to the Second World War – as the threat to these Arcadian frolics. There is a short post-play 'newsreel' which shows the protagonists dealing with the invasion of a weakened France, and the ultimate victory celebrations and reunion of the lovers.

This reading of the play in relation to twentieth-century wars is quite common: it flows from the contrast of the innocent activities of the world depicted in the play (often recognisably mapped onto the British class system) and the demands of real-world masculine performance on the 'officer class'. Not all versions end as positively as Branagh's film: for some productions such as Trevor Nunn's at London's National Theatre in 2003, the 'words of Mercury' are sadly portentous of the deaths of some of the play's characters – including Biron – in the First World War.[13]

Conclusion

Improbable fictions

In many of the plays we have looked at in this book Shakespeare takes an opportunity to theorise, to draw attention to the intellectual and cultural work that is being done at this moment on the stage. Regularly in the comedies (much more so than in the tragedies or histories)[1] the audience is reminded of the artificiality of what is going on on stage; the responsibility is thrown upon us to think, not only about the story, but about its telling, about the human need to make and listen to stories.[2]

Perhaps the most famous instance of this practice is the throw-away line by a minor character, Fabian, in *Twelfth Night* 3.4.109: 'If this were played upon a stage now, I could condemn it as an improbable fiction' – the 'this' in question being Malvolio's transformation into a clown-like parody of a lover. Like Feste, Fabian – who might be thought of as a Shakespearean clown-in-training – speaks wisdom lightly. An *improbable* fiction is exactly what comedy is, at base. The world is not often so kind to us as to produce happy endings out of errors, coincidences, wrong choices in love, miscommunications. Social and political structures do not always guarantee the success of the good-hearted. Nevertheless, we need the 'fictions' that tell us that sometimes

> Jack shall have Jill,
> Naught shall go ill,
> The man shall have his mare again, and all shall be well

– as Puck chants when waking and restoring Lysander to his former love after the midsummer night's dream of irrational desire and pursuit (*Dream* 3.2.461–3).

A Midsummer Night's Dream, like *Love's Labour's Lost* (and *Hamlet*), includes a full-scale performance of a theatrical show within the main play – a stage upon the stage, actors playing actors. Hermia's last line in the main-stage play is, 'Methinks I see these things with parted eye, / When everything seems double' (4.1.186–7). This is a comment like Fabian's, which draws attention to the act of *seeing*, which is central to the audience/stage dynamic, and to the *doubleness* of

138

the audience's perception of the theatrical event: this both feels (emotionally) like the real world and yet is patently an 'improbable fiction'. As Dr Johnson said, audiences always know:

> The truth is, that the spectators are always in their senses, and know, from the first act to the last, that the stage is only a stage, and that the players are only players.
>
> Samuel Johnson, *Preface to Shakespeare* (1765)

Another group of comedies incorporates into their plot structures a metatheatrical consciousness about performance via disguises and deceptions. *Much Ado*'s elaborate masked dance in 2.1, with its teasing and manipulative dialogues, sets the tone for the play's great scenes of deception, both comic (Beatrice and Benedick) and potentially tragic (Hero and Claudio). *As You Like It*'s Rosalind plays on the delicious edge of possible discovery with her cross-gendered performance, as does Viola in *Twelfth Night*, both sustaining the 'improbability' well beyond its necessary adoption; and taking time to let the audience know that this delightful suspense is an important part of the theatrical event.

The two earlier cross-dressed heroines, Julia (*Two Gentlemen of Verona*) and Portia (*The Merchant of Venice*) have somewhat different functions in their plays. Although each heroine comments wittily and with mild bawdiness about her male costume, the disguise is adopted in order to pursue justice rather than as a self-preserving act that then becomes an erotic manoeuvre. That is, these two heroines are 'female heroes' derived from the medieval romance-narratives on which the plays' plots are based. Innogen (*Cymbeline*), the last cross-dressed heroine, is of the same type. Their adventures involve serious social issues: the threat of rape, war, lawlessness, racism and injustice.[3] They come, at times, much closer to tragedy; and, significantly, there is little metatheatrical commentary to be found in these plays.

To return, then, to Biron's task that we glanced at at the beginning of the last chapter – 'To move wild laughter in the face of death' – and apply it to the theatrical experience itself. Shakespeare (through Rosaline) calls the frustration of our conventional expectations of a simple happy ending, whether in the theatre or in the real world, 'impotence', powerlessness. All audiences, however, are at once 'impotent' and empowered. They are at the mercy of the theatrical event: kept in a confined space for the two hours' traffic of the play, but – in a comedy – ultimately they have the power of deciding whether to submit to the players' determination to make us laugh, with jokes, verbal wit, tumbling, pratfalls; to make us hold our breath in suspense; to make us even, occasionally, cry – though they might be tears of happy pathos. It is a continual see-saw, and, at best, gloriously pleasurable. But often the audience's laughter reflex, and their response to the play's improbable fiction, is conditioned by social attitudes that they hold, consciously or otherwise. It is an ongoing challenge for actors and directors to engage with those attitudes. Arguably, it is intellectually dishonest to ignore them and claim that a production is 'traditional' (i.e. quaintly Elizabethan) or 'universal' (set in no particular time and place), though that may be what the audience thinks they want – the safety of the conventional. We all exist in time and history – and to every production of a Shakespearean comedy, whatever it may look like, there will be contemporary meaning.

Further reading

As well as the books mentioned in the notes to each chapter, the following may be useful as a starting-point for further investigations into Shakespearean comedy.

For Shakespeare's life and times: Jonathan Bate, *The Genius of Shakespeare* (London: Picador, 1997); James Shapiro, *1599: A Year in the Life of William Shakespeare* (London: Faber and Faber, 2005); Stephen Greenblatt, *Will in the World: How Shakespeare became Shakespeare* (London: Pimlico, 2005).

For Shakespeare's theatre: Andrew Gurr, *The Shakespearean Stage, 1574–1642*, 3rd edn (Cambridge: Cambridge University Press, 1992); Andrew Gurr, *Playgoing in Shakespeare's London*, 3rd edn (Cambridge: Cambridge University Press, 2004); Tiffany Stern, *Making Shakespeare: From Stage to Page* (London: Routledge, 2004).

For surveys of Shakespeare's comedies: Alexander Leggatt, *Shakespeare's Comedy of Love* (London and New York: Methuen, 1974); Michael Mangan, *A Preface to Shakespeare's Comedies* (London: Longman, 1996); R. W. Maslen, *Shakespeare and Comedy* (London: Thomson Learning, 2006); Alexander Leggatt (ed.), *The Cambridge Companion to Shakespearean Comedy* (Cambridge: Cambridge University Press, 2002).

There are many anthologies of critical essays on the comedies: e.g. Emma Smith (ed.), The Blackwell Guides to Criticism: *Shakespeare's Comedies* (Oxford: Blackwell Publishing, 2004); the Palgrave Macmillan New Casebooks series on individual plays; the Routledge Critical Essays/New Critical Essays series on individual plays. Some of the most stimulating writing about characters in the comedies is to be found in the essays by actors who have performed in them: the Cambridge University Press series *Players of Shakespeare*; the Faber and Faber series *Actors on Shakespeare*.

The best place to start for an overview of critical approaches to each play is the introduction to a scholarly edition: e.g. those published by Cambridge University Press (the New Cambridge Shakespeare, used in this book), Oxford University Press (World's Classics editions), and the Arden Shakespeare. Most of these editions also include some discussion of stage history of the play.

The Cambridge University Press editions of individual plays in the series Shakespeare in Production, which includes many of the comedies, offer a treasure-trove of details about production history with notes describing the details of different performances of each scene.

There is a growing number of books on Shakespeare on film, including a *Cambridge Companion* edited by Russell Jackson (2000); but the number of comedies being filmed has yet to equal the tragedies.

Notes

1 Introduction: comedy as idea and practice

1 John Manningham's Diary, in Geoffrey Bullough, *Narrative and Dramatic Sources of Shakespeare*, II: *The Comedies, 1597–1603* (London: Routledge and Kegan Paul, 1958), 269.

2 Russ McDonald calls such characters 'verbal buffoons', *Shakespeare and the Arts of Language* (Oxford: Oxford University Press, 2001), 122.

3 Louise George Clubb, 'Italian stories on the stage', in Alexander Leggatt (ed.), *The Cambridge Companion to Shakespearean Comedy* (Cambridge: Cambridge University Press, 2002), 35.

4 Louise George Clubb, in *Cambridge Companion*, 36–7. She adds the interesting statistic, 'In eighteen of Scala's forty comedy scenarios the primary *innamorata* puts on boy's clothes, usually to seek the man she loves' (42).

5 Janette Dillon, 'Elizabethan comedy', in *Cambridge Companion*, 51.

6 Janette Dillon, in *Cambridge Companion*, 48–9.

7 Cf. Castiglione, 'In case therefore the Courtier in jesting and speaking merry conceits have a respect to the time, to the persons, to his degree, and not use it too often ... he may be called pleasant and feat conceited [ingenious]' (*The Courtier*, Book 2). Viola of course is conscious of her own need to play the courtier – she does not feel as free as Feste. (For further discussion of Viola's clowning see chapter 5.)

8 Leo Salingar, *Shakespeare and the Traditions of Comedy* (Cambridge: Cambridge University Press, 1974), 257. This book remains the most comprehensive introduction to the origins and historical precursors of Shakespearean comedy.

9 For detailed discussion of the audience of Shakespeare's public theatre, see Andrew Gurr, *The Shakespearean Stage, 1574–1642* (3rd edn, Cambridge: Cambridge University Press, 1992) and *Playgoing in Shakespeare's London* (3rd edn, Cambridge: Cambridge University Press, 2004).

10 Peter Thomson, *Shakespeare's Theatre* (2nd edn, London: Routledge, 1992), 36. Thomson's chapters on Shakespeare's company and its organisation, and the buildings in which it performed, offer a clear and helpful summary of the available evidence. See also Gary Taylor, 'Shakespeare plays on Renaissance stages', in Sarah Stanton and Stanley Wells (eds.), *The Cambridge Companion to Shakespeare on Stage*

(Cambridge: Cambridge University Press, 2002), 1–20, particularly for considerations of casting and costume.

11 Robert Weimann, *Author's Pen and Actor's Voice: Playing and Writing in Shakespeare's Theatre* (Cambridge: Cambridge University Press, 2000), 181.

12 Janette Dillon, 'Shakespeare and the traditions of English stage comedy', in Richard Dutton and Jean E. Howard (eds.), *A Companion to Shakespeare's Works*, III: *The Comedies* (Oxford: Blackwell Publishing, 2003), 4.

13 C. L. Barber, *Shakespeare's Festive Comedy: A Study of Dramatic Form and its Relation to Social Custom* (Princeton, NJ: Princeton University Press, 1959), 3, 7, 8.

14 Northrop Frye, *Anatomy of Criticism: Four Essays* (Princeton, NJ: Princeton University Press, 1957), 166, 182.

15 Jean E. Howard, 'The difficulties of closure: an approach to the problematic in Shakespearean comedy', in A. R. Braunmuller and J. C. Bulman (eds.), *Comedy from Shakespeare to Sheridan* (London: Associated University Presses, 1986), 113, 114. A helpful discussion of the theories of 'festive comedy' is to be found in François Laroque, 'Shakespeare's festive comedies', in Dutton and Howard (eds.), *Companion: Comedies*, 23–46. The essay includes a general survey of clowns and jigs.

16 If Shakespeare did write and publish a sequel to *Love's Labour's Lost* it has disappeared; or it was the alternative title to another comedy of his written about this period – not, however, *The Taming of the Shrew*, as that was listed as a separate play in the other contemporary document that notes the existence of *Love's Labour's Won*. For an authoritative brief account of this mystery, see Stanley Wells and Gary Taylor (eds.), *William Shakespeare: The Complete Works* (Oxford: Oxford University Press, 1988), 309.

2 Farce

1 G. K. Hunter, 'Comedy, farce, romance', in *Comedy from Shakespeare to Sheridan*, A. R. Braunmuller and J. C. Bulman (eds.) (London: Associated University Presses, 1986), 41, 34.

2 Act 4 scene 1 of *Sir Thomas More* (Anon., but including at least one scene probably by Shakespeare) includes a performance at Sir Thomas' house, with some interesting indications about contemporary itinerant players:

> MORE The Marriage of Wit and Wisdom! that, my lads;
> I'll none but that; . . .
> How many are ye?
> PLAYER Four men and a boy, sir.
> MORE But one boy? then I see,
> There's but few women in the play.
> PLAYER Three, my lord; Dame Science, Lady Vanity,
> And Wisdom she herself.
> MORE And one boy play them all? by our Lady, he's laden.

3 See M. A. Katritzky, 'Reading the actress in commedia imagery', in Pamela Allen Brown and Peter Parolin (eds.), *Women Players in England, 1500–1660* (Aldershot: Ashgate, 2005), 109–44, for a summary of recent scholarship on travelling companies that included female performers; see also Brown and Parolin's Introduction for an overview of the issues.

4 The delightful Trevor Nunn musical production (RSC, 1976) even had the Dromios singing versions of these complaints. (This production was televised and is commercially available.)

5 Juan Luis Vives wrote in the early sixteenth century an influential Latin text known as *Instruction of a Christian Woman* (translated into English in 1529). In chapter 12 it includes this passage: 'If thou talk little in company folks think thou canst but little good; if thou speak much they reckon thee light; if thou speak uncunningly, they count thee dull-witted; if thou speak cunningly thou shalt be called a shrew.' (www.press.uillinois.edu/epub/books/vives/) This appears to offer a no-win situation for any young woman!

6   BIONDELLO Where have I been? Nay, how now, where are you? Master, has my fellow Tranio stolen your clothes, or you stolen his, or both? Pray, what's the news?
      LUCENTIO [after a succinct explanation of his disguise] You understand me?
      BIONDELLO Ay, sir. Ne'er a whit.   (1.1.213–15)

The Folio has 'I, sir', which could be inflected by the actor as blank incomprehension. See note in the NCS edition.

7 In Gale Edwards' 1995 production for the RSC this whole sequence was unbearably painful, as Josie Lawrence's Kate became visually isolated (she resembled the broken mannequin on which the dress was modelled), and reduced to begging Grumio for food. For a thought-provoking discussion of this mould-breaking production, see Barbara Hodgdon, 'Katherina bound, or play(K)ating the strictures of everyday life', in *The Shakespeare Trade: Performances and Appropriations* (Philadelphia: University of Pennsylvania Press, 1998), 30–8.

8 Michael Bogdanov's 1978 production for the RSC was a notorious re-reading of the play as a study of abusive male behaviour. See Penny Gay, *As She Likes It: Shakespeare's Unruly Women* (London and New York: Routledge, 1994), for a discussion of the major productions since the Second World War, and the response (or otherwise) to second-wave feminism.

9 The anonymous *Taming of a Shrew*, 1594, does close off the Sly story, waking him up to the real world and sending him off to 'tame' his real wife, a version often used in modern productions. Elizabeth Schafer's *Shakespeare in Production: The Taming of the Shrew* (Cambridge: Cambridge University Press, 2002) offers a thorough discussion of the stage history of the play and a text annotated with details of how individual moments have been performed throughout its history.

10 'Pheasar' may just be a nonsense rhyme; perhaps a combination of 'vizier' and 'geezer'?

11 Falstaff complains about this treatment to Ford via metaphors that signal his sense of himself as a grotesque, food-obsessed body:

> to be stopped in like a strong distillation with stinking clothes that fretted in their own grease. Think of that – a man of my kidney – think of that – that am as subject to heat as butter; a man of continual dissolution and thaw. It was a miracle to 'scape suffocation. And in the height of this bath, when I was more than half stewed in grease like a Dutch dish, to be thrown into the Thames and cooled . . .   (3.5.90–6)

12 Sir Toby Belch in *Twelfth Night*, a paler version of Falstaff, ends by marrying his 'niece's chamber-maid' Maria – another version of the clever 'wife' who can outwit any male.

3 Courtly lovers and the real world

1 'Courtly love', *The New Princeton Encyclopedia of Poetry and Poetics*, Alex Preminger and T. V. F. Brogan (eds.) (Princeton, NJ: Princeton University Press, 1993).
2 For further comment on the courtroom scene, see chapter 7.
3 'Homosociality' as a term in literary criticism was proposed by Eve Kosofsky Sedgwick in *Between Men: English Literature and Male Homosocial Desire* (New York: Columbia University Press, 1985). Discussing Shakespeare's Sonnets, she argues that 'we are in the presence of male heterosexual desire, [but] in the form of a desire to consolidate partnership with authoritative males in and through the bodies of females' (38). This model can also be utilised to help explain the final scene of *Two Gentlemen of Verona*.
4 Antonio, considered realistically, can of course return to the world of mercantile Venice – Portia, that worldly and knowledgeable young woman, brings him the news that his ships are 'richly come to harbour' (5.1.277). He can return to the situation of the play's opening scene, and his lonely life as a merchant.

4 Comedy and language

1 *SOED* gives its sixteenth-century usage, sb. 7: 'A fanciful, ingenious, or witty notion or expression; an affectation of thought or style'.
2 Spoken language was potentially more influential than printing in this period: 'the Stationers' Company, which controlled the printing industry, limited a standard edition to 1250 copies of any one book'. Gabriel Egan, 'Theatre in London', in *Shakespeare: An Oxford Guide*, Stanley Wells and Lena Cowen Orlin (eds.) (Oxford: Oxford University Press, 2003), 24. Since the outdoor theatres could hold up to 3,000 people at a time, ideas and fashions could potentially be rapidly disseminated via theatrical performances.
3 Emma Smith has a brief but illuminating discussion of punning in *The Cambridge Introduction to Shakespeare* (Cambridge: Cambridge University Press, 2007), 77–9.

The whole chapter, 'Language', offers a very readable overview of the issues relevant to Shakespeare's use of language.

4 George Puttenham, *The Arte of English Poesie* (1589), The Third Booke, Of Ornament, ch. IV, Of Language.

5 For details of late Elizabethan language and practice of rhetoric, see Margreta de Grazia, 'Shakespeare and the craft of language', in Margreta de Grazia and Stanley Wells (eds.), *The Cambridge Companion to Shakespeare* (Cambridge: Cambridge University Press, 2001), 49–64. For a more extended discussion, see Russ McDonald, *Shakespeare and the Arts of Language* (Oxford: Oxford University Press, 2001).

6 Quotations from *Love's Labour's Lost* in this chapter are from the Oxford World's Classics edition, ed. G. R. Hibbard (Oxford: Oxford University Press, 1998).

7 For more on Branagh's use of the 'Fred and Ginger' model in his film of *Love's Labour's Lost*, see chapter 7.

8 Their 'betters', typically (as also in *Dream*) behave rudely and patronisingly during the performance. Holofernes, the schoolmaster, rightly reproaches them: 'This is not generous, not gentle, not humble' (5.2.621). The 'gentle'-men have not learnt much humility (i.e. true gentility) at all in the course of their story – all the more reason for the year's trials imposed on them by the ladies.

9 G. R. Hibbard's Introduction to the Oxford World's Classics edition of *Love's Labour's Lost* gives a thorough and entertaining survey of the play's critical and theatrical fortunes.

5 Romantic comedy

1 G. K. Hunter, 'Comedy, farce, romance', in A. R. Braunmuller and J. C. Bulman (eds.), *Comedy from Shakespeare to Sheridan* (London: Associated University Presses, 1986), 41, 43, 45.

2 Barbara Hodgdon offers a thought-provoking reading of Rosalind playing 'a gender of her own' in *The Cambridge Companion to Shakespearean Comedy*, Alexander Leggatt (ed.) (Cambridge: Cambridge University Press, 2002), 190–5; she comments that the performance of '"Rosalind for Ganymed" *is* the play: her role displaces plot with a series of turns or music-hall-like routines' (190). This perception is perhaps reinforced by Rosalind's telling Orlando that she has 'conversed [studied] with a magician' (5.2.48).

3 Catherine Belsey's illuminating discussion of the folk-tale basis of the play, and its intersections with the theory of pastoral and ideas about the performance of gender in the late Elizabethan period, can be found in *Why Shakespeare?* (Basingstoke: Palgrave Macmillan, 2007), 21–41.

4 Janette Dillon comments on Jaques as a clown: both he and Touchstone are 'an addition to Lodge [the author of *Rosalynde*, the play's source-text]; and both characters are named in such a way as to indicate their capacity to stand outside the fiction

as commentators: Jaques with lavatorial innuendo and Touchstone . . . as a testing ground for the pretensions of the other characters, and perhaps of the play itself.' 'Shakespeare and English stage comedy', in *A Companion to Shakespeare's Works*: vol. III, *The Comedies*, Richard Dutton and Jean E. Howard (eds.) (Oxford: Blackwell Publishing, 2003), 8.

5 Hymen is often played by the actor playing one of the shepherds, Corin or William – elaborately disguised as a god or simply as the shepherd in his best clothes and appropriately garlanded.

6 Catherine Belsey writes perceptively about riddling and 'old tales' in *Twelfth Night* in *Why Shakespeare?*, ch. 7. See also Penny Gay, '*Twelfth Night*: "The babbling gossip of the air"', in Dutton and Howard (eds.), *A Companion to Shakespeare's Works*, 429–43.

7 Actors can take the opportunity to address the audience in this solo scene – thus further positioning Malvolio as a clown. See Donald Sinden's description of his techniques for performing this scene, *Players of Shakespeare*, Philip Brockbank (ed.) (Cambridge: Cambridge University Press, 1985), 41–66.

6 Problematic plots and endings: clowning and comedy post-*Hamlet*

1 'Clown' and 'Other' are the speech headings given in the Folio and used in the New Cambridge Shakespeare edition. This indicates that one actor was the company's professional clown, the 'other' simply one of its versatile adult actors.

2 This definition of a 'Phantasticke' is given in Thomas Overbury's *Characters* (1614), cited in the New Cambridge Shakespeare edition of the play, 87.

3 For a definition and discussion of homosociality, see chapter 3, note 3.

4 Steven Mentz, 'Revising the sources: novella, romance, and the meanings of fiction in *All's Well, That Ends Well*', in *All's Well, That Ends Well: New Critical Essays*, Gary Waller (ed.) (London and New York: Routledge, 2007), 58. 'Novella' is a term for the more bawdy short fictions of the Middle Ages and Renaissance, 'romance' signifies high-minded courtly adventures. Shakespeare's sources for many comedies (and tragedies) included both romances and novellas.

5 For a helpful overview of the way Shakespeare uses the conventions of genre – and disregards them – see Susan Snyder, 'The genres of Shakespeare's plays', in Margreta de Grazia and Stanley Wells (eds.), *The Cambridge Companion to Shakespeare* (Cambridge: Cambridge University Press, 2001), 83–98.

6 Modern directors are often anxious about this sudden shift to comedy, and bring on the bear as a sinister and/or monstrous figure: for example, as a looming shadow projected onto the stage, engulfing Antigonus; or – in a memorable production by Michael Pennington in 1990 – as Leontes, a black-clad figure, wearing a bear-claw on the hand that taps Antigonus on the shoulder. These decisions, however, only delay the rapid change of mood for a few seconds: the comic Old Shepherd's entry follows immediately.

7 Compare the stage direction, 'Clock strikes', and Olivia's comment on it, 'The clock upbraids me with the waste of time', at the halfway point of *Twelfth Night* (3.1.115).

7 The afterlives of Shakespeare's comedies

1 A possible clue to the identification of Shakespeare and Biron is that Biron is an accomplished sonneteer; in the course of the play his dialogue includes seven partial or complete sonnets, including one on 'black beauty' that reads like an alternative version of Sonnet 127 (4.3.255–62).
2 For the formula 'improbable fictions' see Conclusion.
3 As early as 1709 Nicholas Rowe, in his edition of Shakespeare's complete works, wrote: 'though we have seen that play received and acted as a comedy, and the part of the Jew performed by an excellent comedian, yet I cannot but think it was designed tragically by the author'. Rowe quoted in Emma Smith (ed.), *Shakespeare's Comedies*, Blackwell Guides to Criticism (Oxford: Blackwell, 2004), 7.
4 Jane Austen, *Letters*, ed. Deirdre Le Faye (3rd edn, Oxford University Press, 1995), 6 March 1814.
5 Elizabeth Schafer, Introduction, *Shakespeare in Production: The Taming of the Shrew* (Cambridge: Cambridge University Press, 2002), 6–7.
6 For detailed discussion of the various choices made by actors and directors through-out the twentieth-century performance of the play, and in films, see Schafer, *passim*; also Penny Gay, *As She Likes It: Shakespeare's Unruly Women* (London and New York: Routledge, 1994), 86–119. See also Barbara Hodgdon, 'Katherina bound, or play(K)ating the strictures of everyday life', in *The Shakespeare Trade: Performances and Appropriations* (Philadelphia: University of Pennsylvania Press, 1998), 1–38.
7 George C. D. Odell, *Shakespeare from Betterton to Irving*, 2 vols. (1920, repr. New York: Dover Publications, 1966), I, 228.
8 These details are from the playbill reproduced in Odell I, 262–3.
9 The basic question for any production of *Much Ado* is: what visual conventions (i.e. what 'period') can unify the lovers, the military, and the clownish working-class, and make the extravagant goings-on of the plot convincing? It must be a society in which gentry behaviour is ruled by strict conventions, especially regarding gender – but which tolerates the efforts to maintain their freedom of two people who think themselves outside these conventions. See Gay, *As She Likes It*, and John F. Cox, *Shakespeare in Production: Much Ado About Nothing* (Cambridge: Cambridge University Press, 1997), for accounts of the different periods in which productions have been set in theatrical productions.
10 Kenneth Branagh, *Much Ado About Nothing / by William Shakespeare*: Screenplay, introduction, and notes on the making of the film (London: Chatto and Windus, 1993), xiv.
11 It should be noted, however, that Samuel Phelps' production at Sadler's Wells (1853) eschewed wings and white muslin, showing fairies that were 'real, intangible,

shadowy beings' (Odell II, 324, quoting Douglas Jerrold). Phelps obtained his magical effects through unprecedented attention to lighting and use of a gauze scrim.

12 Details of the musical and textual additions in Reynolds' *Comedy of Errors* can be found in Odell II, 131–5.

13 'The action begins with a deafening, bewildering First World War battle scene. This, you realise with a start, is the hero Berowne's [Biron's] present reality. But as the wounded, possibly dying, man lies on the battlefield, his mind flashes back to that last golden summer before the Great War, with the rest of the action set in the grounds of a great English country house.' As a further example of film's cultural potency, the critic goes on to note, 'It was an inspired idea to cast Joseph Fiennes as Berowne. The actor is best known for his performance in the title role of *Shakespeare in Love*, and if we have a self-portrait of the young Shakespeare, Berowne is surely it. He is witty, cynical, self-mocking, but with an ardour and tenderness about him too, qualities all superbly caught by Fiennes.' Charles Spencer, *Daily Telegraph*, 22 February 2003.

Conclusion

1 The major examples of theatrical self-consciousness in the histories would include the Chorus in *Henry V* and the Players in *Hamlet*. Both plays date from the first seasons of performances at the new Globe theatre, when Shakespeare's company was probably in confident and self-congratulatory mood.

2 See Catherine Belsey, *Why Shakespeare?* (Basingstoke: Palgrave Macmillan, 2007) for an argument about the importance of story in Shakespeare. Belsey particularly stresses the folk-tale origins of many of the plays.

3 See Barbara Hodgdon, *The Cambridge Companion to Shakespearean Comedy*, for a slightly different reading of the cross-dressed heroines' relation to social issues. The basic point (with which I agree) is that 'each play tailors sexual disguise to its own sociocultural milieu and gender politics' – Portia is, in Hodgdon's terms, clearly the most 'feminist' of the cross-dressed heroines, 'one who leaves a household where she is "master" to take up a similarly powerful role in the public sphere' (185). But, as I commented in chapter 3, she must be disguised as a young man to achieve this.

Index